*Facet
Theory*

Advanced Quantitative Techniques in the Social Sciences

Facet
Theory
Form and
Content

Ingwer Borg
Samuel Shye

Advanced Quantitative Techniques
in the Social Sciences Series **5**

SAGE Publications
International Educational and Professional Publisher
Thousand Oaks London New Delhi
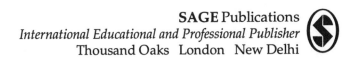

For information address:

 SAGE Publications, Inc.
2455 Teller Road
Thousand Oaks, California 91320

SAGE Publications Ltd.
6 Bonhill Street
London EC2A 4PU
United Kingdom

SAGE Publications India Pvt. Ltd.
M-32 Market
Greater Kailash I
New Delhi 110 048 India

Printed in the United States of America

Library of Congress Cataloging-in-Publication Data

Borg, Ingwer.
  Facet theory: form and content / Ingwer Borg, Samuel Shye.
      p.   cm.—(Advanced quantitative techniques in the social
  sciences; 5)
    Includes bibliographical references and index.
    ISBN 0-8039-4756-9 (alk. paper)
    1. Social sciences—Methodology. I. Shye, Samuel. II. Title.
  III. Series.
  H61.B626 1995
  300'.72—dc20   95-6840

This book is printed on acid-free paper.

95 96 97 98 99 10 9 8 7 6 5 4 3 2 1

Sage Production Editor: Astrid Virding
Sage Typesetter: Andrea D. Swanson

Contents

Series Editor's Introduction

This book by Borg and Shye is quite different from other books in the series. Facet theory is original, because it links social science theory, design of studies, and analysis of the data in a very intricate way. As Borg and Shye explain, facet theory is a "methodological approach," which means that it is not just a family of data analysis techniques. Comparable "frameworks" are Fisher's theory of experimental design (with strong links to the analysis of variance), Wold's approach to soft modeling (using partial least squares regressions), and the Luce-Suppes-Krantz-Tversky approach to measurement (although this last framework mostly hovers above the social and behavioral sciences, without really touching them).

Facet theory originates with Louis Guttman. Over a period of more than 40 years, Guttman has contributed many of the basic building blocks and frameworks of the current quantitative social and behavioral sciences. Anybody with any knowledge of the field of quantitative social and behavioral research will have no difficulty identifying Guttman as by far the most influential and original contributor. He invented scale analysis, laying the foundations for much of latent structure and latent trait theory. This resulted in his 1941 paper introducing multiple correspondence analysis in full detail. Factor analysis never recovered from the fundamental contributions Guttman made over a period of 20 years. In the 1950s and

1960s, he worked, in relative isolation, on nonmetric scaling techniques, applying them to various forms of categorical data structures. In a sense, Guttman's contributions are all incorporated in the framework of facet theory.

Facet theory provides social and behavioral scientists with a language to talk about their domains of discourse, and to structure and analyze the instruments they use to study this domain. In a sense, it is a rather idiosyncratic approach, because it relies heavily on a specific language that not many people outside the International Facet Theory Society are using. But of course Fisher's approach to agricultural experiments was probably idiosyncratic as well, until everybody started using the language of randomization and blocking. The mapping sentence approach of facet theory, coupled with the heavily geometric and nonlinear representations of SSA and MSA, is an interesting alternative to some of the existing frameworks in quantitative social science. In particular, it seems to me that it comes up with interesting results in the fields of attitude and intelligence measurement, in the areas usually subjected to LISREL and friends, and in the wasteland of factor analysis.

One problem with facet theory is that there has not been an introductory text or textbook available, although many applications have been published illustrating the use of the methodology. This book by Borg and Shye fills this gap, and it does it in a clear and comprehensive way.

JAN DE LEEUW

Preface

Facet theory (FT) is primarily a methodological approach for the social sciences, but it is also closely related to particular contents that FT helped to unfold and that, in turn, have helped to develop FT. To look at FT as a mere tool would not only be sterile but also unmotivated. We have used in this book a number of examples, not only to illustrate methodological points, but also to demonstrate how facet-theoretical thinking and theory construction naturally develop out of substantive questions. The examples were chosen so as to be reasonably interesting and intelligible to any social scientist.

As is true for any methodology, the principle of learning-by-doing also holds—particularly so because of its involvement with "content"—for FT. Starting from a substantive question and thinking about it more carefully, one is naturally led to various distinctions that can be formalized as facets. In the social sciences, this typically means predicting that certain person types will exhibit certain patterns of behavior in certain classes of situations. In that typologies, classifications, differentiation of patterns, and so forth, are a natural result of any systematic thinking, any scientific theory construction automatically has facet-theoretical elements. The realization, however, that one uses facet theory anyway (as one uses prose), offers little of practical use. The FT method aims, above all, at *explicating the implicit.* Experience has shown that this leads to considerable conceptual clarity and control. Using FT, even students in their first semesters conceive differentiated constructs and interesting hypotheses. The technique of explication also enables one to see new and substantively important regularities in data already published in the literature but analyzed mechanically with standard statistical tools.

FT, in essence, consists of two major components: FT design and FT data analysis. These two blocks are linked by correspondence hypotheses. As a design methodology, FT comprises experimental design and sample construction as special cases. As far as data analysis is concerned, FT is a flexible methodology, admitting, in principle, methods such as factor analysis, structural equation modeling, cluster analysis, conjoint measurement, analysis of variance, regression analysis and, in particular, discriminant analysis. These techniques are, however, often more "extrinsic" for the scientific purpose of an inquiry (i.e., for establishing empirical laws) than procedures developed within the FT context. The reader, in any case, will not be pushed to forget everything he or she knows and analyze his or her data only with a particular method or computer program. We will try, though, to focus more attention on the question of whether a given data analysis method is apt to answer the questions that the researcher really asks of the data. The typically soft methods of FT work with few restrictions and assumptions, so that the substantive findings do not become loaded with mathematical structures and constraints that are irrelevant to the studied domain. Moreover, FT methods typically pay little attention to statistical inference, but concentrate more on issues relevant for successive approximation, cumulative data modeling, and the establishment of scientific laws. Thus, they are geared toward replicability, generalizability, and cumulative theory construction ("intrinsic data analysis").

Hard models evolve in FT in a natural, bottom-up way. Facets are introduced to structure originally monolithic constructs. These facets are then interconnected in a mapping sentence. The mapping sentence is improved in different partnerships that involve the construction of concrete items and the analysis of the facets' correspondences to properties of pertinent data. Facets may be dropped, modified, or extended; further facets may be added to account for additional variance, and so forth. With sharply defined facets and an enhanced technicality of the facets' interconnections, mapping sentences become, in effect, mathematical models.

The natural way to read this book is in a sequential manner. Readers who know little or nothing about FT should start by reading Chapter 1. To get more of the flavor of FT, it might be helpful to screen several areas of substantive interest (see index "applications/results") before continuing reading systematically.

This book contains twelve chapters. Briefly, they address the following topics. Chapter 1 introduces FT by discussing an example. As in almost all other examples in this book, we selected this example because it is reasonably interesting to all social scientists; it appeared previously in the literature and, thus, can be studied there in more detail; it deals with a real-world problem, not just with an illustrative set of artificial data; it serves to introduce a variety of issues that are dealt with further in subsequent chapters. The introductory example is concerned with facets of duration judgments. The question is studied in the framework of a traditional factorial design; therefore, the reader can see how such a familiar scheme relates to FT and what data-analytical perspectives (besides ANOVA) can be chosen for looking at such data.

Chapter 2 gives a very compact overview of the elements of FT: FT as a design methodology, FT as a set of particular data analytical methods, and FT as a system of correspondence hypotheses that link the observations made within a given design to properties of the definitional system. The chapter illustrates how these elements are interrelated and how they relate to other notions of theory construction and statistics.

Chapter 3 clarifies what is meant by observations and what role facets play in this context. This chapter shows that observations always involve three basic sets: persons, questions, and admissible answers to them. These sets are related to each other by means of an (observational) mapping.

Chapter 4 shows that facets are intimately related to relations, particularly to equivalence relations. Stratification of a population by facets when constructing a representative sample is a well-known example. The same idea is applied to the set of questions and responses. A number of issues that are of great practical importance in this context are addressed: how to find good facets, how to generate question types by facets, how to systematically construct or cull concrete items on this basis, and so forth. These questions, in turn, bring up various abstract issues such as whether one should use obtrusive questions in the sense of Rossi's vignettes or unobtrusive ones; or whether classifying questions by facets means that one formulates a hypothesis or a definition. The chapter ends by distinguishing two basic forms of mapping sentences, categorical and structioned ones. Such mapping sentences are key devices for FT-related theory construction, as well as for very practical issues such as systematic item construction.

Chapter 5 discusses mapping sentences in more detail. It illustrates how mapping sentences arise in practice, how they naturally guide cumulative research, and how they can be made more precise by formalizing their language so that, finally, they represent mathematical models arising out of content in a bottom-up process.

Chapter 6 introduces the notion of common range. A common range is usually the starting point of designing a mapping sentence. An example is discussed in which two such mapping sentence are constructed, and then pulled together by finding a common meaning to their ranges.

Chapter 7 addresses items which, in FT, are defined as questions together with their admissible answers. Two particularly important classes of items, attitude and intelligence items, are discussed in detail, including "principal components" of attitudes. The FT approach to construct item batteries is contrasted with the exploratory and the item-analytical method.

Chapter 8 gives a concise overview of several principles on which correspondence hypotheses relating FT design to observations are built. One example is to "explain" the data by regressing them on the facets of the design. Another principle is a discrimination hypothesis that states that conceptual distinctions made in the definitional system are mirrored in corresponding differences in the data. A particularly successful variety of this principle is the class of regional hypotheses for geometric representations of the data.

Chapter 9 discusses bivariate regression hypotheses for items of one or of different universes, respectively. A particular class of such hypotheses is known as laws of monotonicity. Laws of monotonicity for attitudes and for intelligence, confirmed in hundreds of empirical studies, are the best known examples. They predict that, under reasonable conditions, items pertaining to the specified content universe should correlate positively among each other.

Chapter 10 discusses how to analyze data profiles. A very general method is multidimensional scalogram analysis or multidimensional structuple analysis (MSA). MSA attempts to represent the data profiles by points in a space so that this space can be partitioned by each item in accordance with its measurement categories. Another method is partial order scalogram analysis or partial order structuple analysis (POSA). Some connections of POSA to conjoint measurement are outlined. Then, an important special case of POSA, POSAC, is introduced formally and by way of illustration.

Chapter 11 deals with another aspect of the data that is associated with a data analysis method called smallest space analysis, multidimensional similarity structure analysis or multidimensional scaling (SSA, MDS). SSA represents similarity coefficients (typically correlation coefficients for sets of items) as distances among points in a multidimensional space. The FT way to "interpret" such an SSA space is to look for a correspondence between the properties of the items and regions of the points that represent them in the SSA space. Particular classes of such regional patterns that often arise in practice (such as a simplex, circumplex, radex, or multiplex) are discussed and illustrated by examples. Practical questions (such as how to look at higher-dimensional spaces) as well as theoretical issues (falsifiability of regional hypotheses, post-hoc partitionings, replicability, etc.) are addressed in detail. A method for objectively partitioning an SSA space, Faceted SSA, is introduced. Then, regional hypothesis testing for SSA spaces is compared to other methods such as cluster analysis, factor analysis, multitrait multimethod method (MTMM), and structural equation modeling (LISREL). It is found that all of these methods are based on assumptions about the structural correspondence of content and data that usually cannot be justified. Moreover, it is shown that findings by methods such as factor analysis are quite dependent on the particular sampling of items from the content universe, whereas SSA is robust in this sense. Then, a number of patterns that were shown to result with lawful regularity in practice (such as the *complexity* facet in intelligence tests), can only be seen in SSA, not, for example, in factor analysis.

Chapter 12, finally, addresses a number of issues that are often asked in practice when discussing FT or when presenting papers that build on FT. Such issues are concerned with FT and measurement, FT and significance tests, FT and hard sciences, constructing "indexes" using FT, and so forth.

The authors would like to thank James C. Steiger (University of British Columbia, Canada) and, in particular, Peter Swanborn (University of Amsterdam, The Netherlands) for constructive criticism of a previous manuscript.

An Introductory Example

- Design
- Observations
- Analysis of Variance
- Partial Order
- Multidimensional Similarity Structure Analysis

Let us begin with an example from psychological research to establish an intuitive understanding of facet theory (FT). The question that is studied here is, what do people believe about the subjective duration of different situations? Do they, for example, believe that time drags more at the office than at a party? This seems plausible, no doubt, but exactly what properties of the situation determine such judgments?

Design

In experimental investigations, a number of properties of a situation have been shown, singly, to have an effect on judgments of duration of time. A situation is felt to be relatively brief if it is pleasant, if many things are happening, if its events are not monotonous, and if coping with it is difficult. It seems natural to assume that these facets should also influence symbolic duration judgments, that is, duration judgments on hypothetical situations. In any case, one could define situations that differ on these facets and then see how people rate them in terms of subjective duration. We express this as follows:[1]

1

Positivity
	(	$p1$ = pleasant	)	
Person (p) believes that a	(	$p2$ = neutral	)	situation with
	(	$p3$ = unpleasant	)	

Number	Variability		Difficulty	
($m1$ = many)	($v1$ = variable	)	($s1$ = difficult)	
( )	(	) events that are	(	) to handle
($m2$ = few)	($v2$ = monotonous	)	($s2$ = easy)	

Reaction
	(	very short in duration	)
are felt as　→	(	to	)
	(	very long in duration	)

This *mapping sentence* first contains a place holder for person p. That is, p could be replaced by "Jim Smith" or "Karen Jones," for example. Then, the situation is characterized by four aspects, characteristics, or *facets*: *positivity of events, number of events, variability of events,* and *difficulty in handling events.* With the number of facet elements we have specified here—3 on positivity, 2 on number, 2 on variability, and 2 on difficulty—we have $3 \times 2 \times 2 \times 2 = 24$ different situation types. They are characterized by their *structuples,* that is, the combination of facet elements taken one from each facet. Thus, for example, the situation ($p3$, $m2,v1,s2$) or, for short, 3212 is defined to be an unpleasant one (the first digit, 3, corresponds to $p3$ = unpleasant), in which few things are happening (the 2 in the second place of the structuple) with variability (the 1 in the third place), and no problems with which to cope (the 2 in the last place). Each facet element in the structuple is called a *struct.* Table 1.1 lists the structuples for all 24 situations. (Structuples are also referred to in the literature as *profiles.* If, as it is true in the present case, the structuples are formed from conceptual elements, we speak of *content structuples.*)

Our interest here is how some (not further specified) sample of people judge the duration of these situation types. Expressed differently, we ask how persons "map" the situations onto the response scale. This is indicated by the little arrow in the mapping sentence: To its left, we have the conditions of the observation (persons, stimuli); to its right, the range of possible observations or data.

The mapping sentence is a design for certain observations. The 24 situation types that it identifies are, however, quite abstract and cannot be presented directly as stimuli to people. Hence, for each situation type, a

TABLE 1.1 Twenty-Four Situation Types With Structuples and Mean Empirical Duration Ratings[a]

Situation	Structuple	Mean Duration
1	1212	3.29
2	2112	3.54
3	1221	3.87
4	1112	3.90
5	1122	3.95
6	1111	4.00
7	2212	4.03
8	2121	4.05
9	1121	4.37
10	1211	4.41
11	2211	4.42
12	1222	4.43
13	3111	4.46
14	2111	4.54
15	2122	4.57
16	3121	4.57
17	2221	4.66
18	3112	4.70
19	3211	4.93
20	3221	4.94
21	3122	5.00
22	2222	5.08
23	3212	5.15
24	3222	5.67

SOURCE: Galinat & Borg (1987).
NOTE: a. Greater values indicate longer duration.

concrete case was constructed. The following story illustrates Situation 4 (1112):

> You are playing a simple card game with your children. It is quite easy for you to win this game because your kids are not serious opponents. The game requires you to exchange many different cards. The game is fun throughout the 3 minutes that it lasts.

This description is supplemented by the question: What do you think, how long would this card game seem to last? Would it seem longer or shorter than 3 minutes?

Observations

Seventy-six people rated this and 23 other hypothetical situations on a
7-point scale from 1 *a lot shorter* to 7 *a lot longer.* This bipolar scale,
together with the question, What do you think, how long . . . last?, is a
concrete specification for the generic response range *very long . . . very
short* in duration in the above mapping sentence. Table 1.1 exhibits the
ratings that were observed for these items on the average.

Analysis of Variance

The plan of this study is a factorial design: The experimental "factors"
or independent variables are the four facets, the dependent variable is the
duration judgment. The usual data analysis for such data is analysis of
variance (ANOVA). It shows that the facets' positivity, variability, and
number have a significant effect on the duration ratings, whereas difficulty
has not. Furthermore, some two-way interactions and the four-way interaction are also significant (Galinat & Borg, 1987).

The direction of the simple effects can be seen from the values in Table
1.1. Situations that are thought to be pleasant ($p1$) are rated, on the average,
as 4.03 on the duration scale, whereas unpleasant ones ($p3$) are rated 4.93.
The neutral situations are in between with a mean score of 4.36. The effects
of the other facets also lie in the expected direction.

One could have tested such directed hypotheses in the first place, but
ANOVA is not suited for this. It merely asks whether certain means differ
from each other. Moreover, ANOVA adds what we like to ask a number of
"assumptions" (such as interval scale level for the dependent variable,
additive conjunction of the effects, normal distribution of errors, etc.)
whose nature is more formal-mathematical than psychological-theoretical.
Thus, ANOVA is a data analysis procedure that is rather *extrinsic* to our
substantive question. As a consequence, it is difficult to say, for example,
whether interaction effects are caused by the subjects' judgments or the
mathematical constraints imposed onto the data.

Partial Order

Let us now also consider a more *intrinsic* data analysis whose restrictions are largely derived from substantive considerations formulated in the

previous mapping sentence. We first note that its four facets are each ordered in the same sense. If we use the symbol > to denote the (definitional) relation "more interesting," then we have pleasant > neutral > unpleasant, many > few, variable > monotonous, and difficult > easy.[2] From these orders, we can establish a partial order for all situation types: situations of type x should be rated as more interesting than those of type y, if at least one struct of x is more interesting than the corresponding struct of y, and no struct is less interesting than its counterpart in y. If one x-struct is more interesting than the corresponding struct of y, whereas another x-struct is less interesting than its counterpart in y, then the situations cannot be compared without making further assumptions. For Situations 10 and 20 we should expect that the former is rated as more interesting because, for the respective structuples (Table 1.1), it holds that 1211 has more interesting structs than 3221 on the first and third position, whereas the second and fourth structs are equal. Written in more detail, the comparison reads as follows:

$$(\quad p1, m2, v1, s1 \quad) \; = \; (\quad \text{pleasant}, \quad \text{few}, \quad \text{variable}, \quad \text{difficult} \quad)$$
$$(\quad p3, m2, v2, s1 \quad) \; = \; (\quad \text{unpleasant}, \quad \text{few}, \quad \text{monotonous}, \text{difficult} \quad)$$

Thus, 1211 is coded as more interesting than 3221 because $p1 > p3$, $2 = 2$, $v1 > v2$, and $1 = 1$. But it is not defined by how much it is more interesting. Neither is it defined whether 1222 is more—or less—interesting than 3211. (Such statements would require further specifications concerning the relative weights of the facet elements.)

The definitions imply a partial order of situation types, represented by the *Hasse diagram* in Figure 1.1. The italicized numbers represent the situation types from Table 1.1; the four-digit numbers, structuples. Situations connected by descending paths are comparable in the sense of the above logic; that is, if two situations are thus connected, one of them is defined as more interesting than the other.

Our hypothesis was that if one situation is more interesting than another, then it would be perceived as relatively short in duration. The lines are solid where the mean duration ratings from Table 1.1 do correspond to such predictions; dashed, where they do not. We see, for example, that Situation 13 is connected to 18 by a solid path, because (a) they are comparable and (b) the duration score for Situation 13 is 4.46, which is shorter than the one for Situation 18, which is 4.70.

Errors of prediction are concentrated mostly within the short situations. There are many potential causes for such errors. Possibly the ANOVA was right after all in pointing to interactions; or an important facet is missing

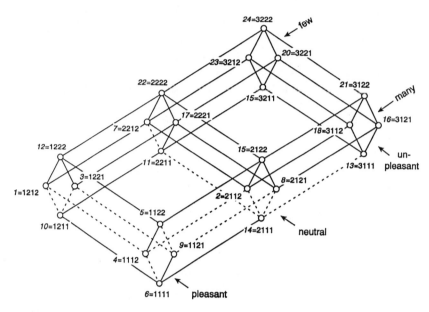

Figure 1.1. Hasse Diagram of Situations From Table 1.1

NOTE: Solid lines indicate where order predictions of structuples (shown in parentheses) are empirically satisfied; broken lines, where they are violated.

from our design and thus remains uncontrolled; or the operationalization of the structuples through our little stories was inappropriate, unreliable, or introduced further uncontrolled effects; or it is simply more difficult for the respondents to distinguish reliably among the shorter situations.

Multidimensional Similarity Structure Analysis

Data can always be looked at in different ways. It is often less interesting to ask how strongly different facets affect a dependent variable than to check whether they show up in the structure of the observations. To illustrate such a question, we look at the correlations among the 24 different stimuli. We represent these correlations geometrically so that each situation corresponds to a point in space. The closer the points are to each other, the higher the correlation of the duration judgments for the situations. A procedure that yields such a representation is *multidimensional similarity structure analysis* (SSA or MDS) (Borg & Lingoes, 1987; Guttman, 1968; Kruskal, 1964).

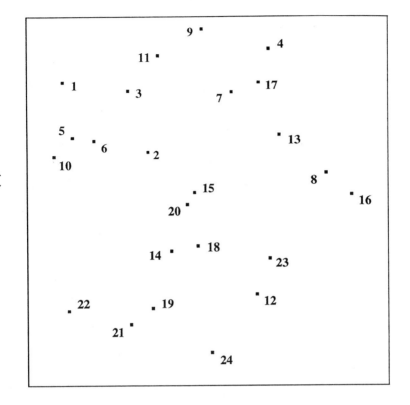

DIM(2)

Figure 1.2. Projection Plane of SSA Configuration, Spanned by the First Two Principal Components

In this procedure, we look at a four-dimensional SSA space through some of its projection planes. Figure 1.2 shows the plane spanned by the first two principal axes of the SSA configuration, Dim(1) and Dim(2). The point indexes correspond to the 24 situations in Table 1.1. Figure 1.3 shows the same point configuration but with different labels: These show the element that each point has on the first facet (*facet diagram*). For example, instead of *24* in Figure 1.2, we have a *neg* in Figure 1.3, because situation 24 was defined as 3 = *p*3 = unpleasant. (Instead of neg, one could also have chosen *p*3, unpleasant, −, 3, or any other symbolism.)

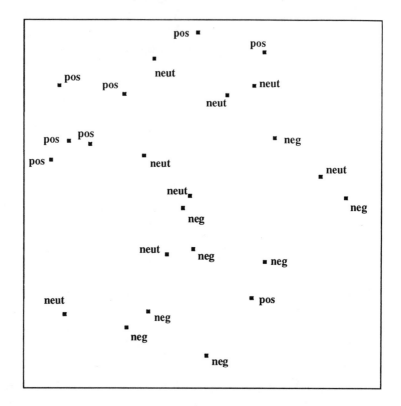

DIM(2)

Figure 1.3. Facet Diagram Over Figure 1.2 for the Facet Positivity

In Figure 1.3, one notes immediately that the points marked as *pos, neut,* and *neg,* respectively, are not distributed randomly. Rather, the plane can be cut (*partitioned*) into regions so that each region contains only, or almost only, points of one particular type. Figure 1.4 shows such a partition. It contains two minor errors—Points 8 and 13 do not quite lie in the regions where they "should" lie but they are not far from the boundaries of those regions—and one gross error—that is, Point 12. Figure 1.5 represents an alternative partition that is error free. This partition depends heavily, however, on the position of Point 12 (marked by an arrow in Figure 1.5) and, therefore, may be less reliable in empirical replications of the study. Moreover, the two partitions

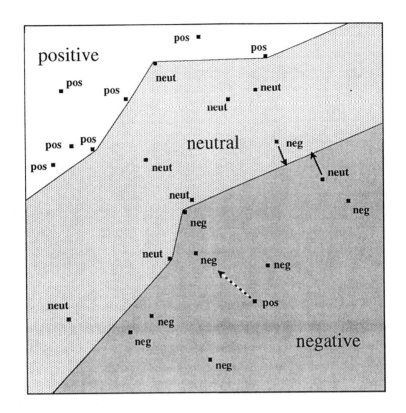

DIM(2)

Figure 1.4. Partitioning of Figure 1.3 by Roughly Straight Lines Into "Positive," "Neutral," and "Negative" Regions
NOTE: Arrows indicate errors of placement.

imply different things. The concentric regions of Figure 1.5 predict that the duration ratings on unpleasant situations should correlate higher among each other, on average, than those for pleasant situations. The parallel regions of Figure 1.4 do not thus restrict the correlations.

Nevertheless, the two partitions are similar in splitting the plane into *ordered* regions, in which the neutral region lies in between the positive and the negative ones. Hence, the regions are ordered as the facet positivity itself. Neither the spatial organization induced by the straight lines nor that

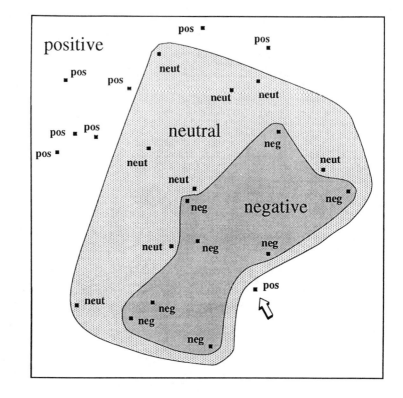

Figure 1.5. Partitioning of Figure 1.3 by Concentric Lines
NOTE: Arrow indicates "critical" points.

induced by concentric circular lines would, therefore, have problems in accommodating a positivity facet that distinguishes many more than just three levels. This is important because what is wanted, eventually, is not a theory about some 24 concrete stimuli but about the *universe* of such situation types. Consequently, we see that the facet positivity is reflected in the structure of the universe of duration items. The decision on which of the two partitions is ultimately correct, requires further data.

Figure 1.6 shows another plane of the SSA space that is orthogonal to the one exhibited in Figures 1.3 through 1.5. This plane is spanned by the

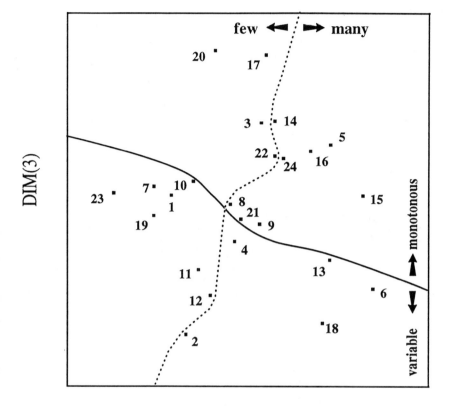

Figure 1.6. Plane Spanned by Third and Fourth Principal Component of SSA Configuration, Including the Partitions of the Facets Number (vertical line) and Variability

principal Axes 3 and 4 of the SSA configuration. One recognizes from the respective facet diagrams that this configuration can be partitioned by the facet number—without error—and also by variability—with two errors. The facet difficulty is not reflected in the SSA configuration; that is, the points representing easy and difficult situations, respectively, seem to be so scrambled that they cannot be discriminated by any but the most irregular partitions. Such partitions are, however, rarely useful because they are unlikely to be replicated.

SSA thus shows that the structure of the duration ratings can, in a way, be explained by three of the four facets of the design. This explanation is, moreover, compatible with considerations that extend beyond the sample of the given 24 concrete situations and relate to their universe. With the partitions shown in Figures 1.4 and 1.6, one arrives at an embryonic Cartesian coordinate system spanned by the three facets positivity, number, and variability. Another coordinate system is suggested if we accept the circular partition shown in Figure 1.5. In this case, we have some evidence for a polar coordinate system of these facets.

Notes

1. In facets and mapping sentences, we usually write indexes not as subscripts but on the same line. That is, instead of p_1 we write $p1$. This is typographically much simpler and normally does not lead to ambiguities.

2. The term *interesting* (etymologically: it matters, makes a difference) is suitable because it suggests quantity of relevant events—quantity of events relevant to one's wants and needs (the positivity facet), quantity of relevantly different events (the number facet), quantity of relevantly different kinds of events (the variability facet), and quantity of different relations (and levels of relations) among events (the difficulty facet).

2 Basic Elements of Facet Theory

- Design, Data, and Correspondence Hypotheses
- FT as a Theory

Design, Data, and Correspondence Hypotheses

The introductory example illustrates three features of facet theory: design, data analysis, and hypotheses of correspondence between the two. These features serve the purposes of defining a domain of interest, explicating its structure, guiding data collection, choosing an appropriate data analytic procedure, and helping to build a theory for this domain.

The *design* in facet theory is aimed at promoting the level of formality in defining the domain of interest and explicating its structure, thereby serving as a basis for systematic data collection. Facet design of the investigated domain explicitly specifies concepts and contexts that guide the empirical observations. As in experimental design or survey sampling, which can be considered special cases of FT, one is further interested in whether and how the different conceptual distinctions show up in empirical data.

Data analysis in FT does not exclude traditional (e.g., linear) statistical procedures. Such procedures often arise as special cases of FT's "softer" procedures. One notes, for example, that the duration data in Chapter 1 could also be analyzed by using regression analysis with the facets as predictor variables. Indeed, this type of analysis shows that facets F1, F2, and F4 all have significant effects on the duration judgments. The statistical model employed by regression analysis is, however, quite restrictive and assumes that the duration ratings are a linear combination of the design facets.

Procedures that involve constraints and specifications that are not inherent to the data definitions (design)—for example, linear statistical models for data that, by design, are ordinal—are considered *extrinsic* in FT. *Intrinsic* procedures (Guttman, 1982c, 1982d), in contrast, closely adhere to the defining features of the data. The extrinsic-intrinsic distinction is, however, not equivalent to the usual uniqueness or scale level notion. It involves "four varieties of primacy" (Guttman, 1982c):

> . . . purpose, inclusion, logic, and revocability. These four varieties may have an order among themselves, with purpose being the most intrinsic. Many varieties of primacy can be suggested beyond the present four. And more than one variety may apply to the same concept. (p. 1)

Given that the purpose of science is to establish empirical laws, intrinsic procedures pay attention to general principles for cumulative theory construction such as robustness of structural findings and the possibility to closely link empirical regularities to facets of the design. Formally, each extrinsic model can be expressed as a special case of an intrinsic model (inclusion). Cluster analysis, for example, can be seen as a special case of SSA in that clusters are special cases of regions. Faceted SSA, which interlocks the formal SSA representation problem more closely with design facets by representing similarity coefficients as distances as it places the points such that the space can be partitioned optimally to reflect the points' classifications on the design facets (Guttman, 1976) or by optimally partitioning a given SSA space in the same sense (Shye, 1991a), is even more intrinsic because it assesses correspondences between definitional features of the observations and their empirical structure (purpose).

A strategic shift in focus from the extrinsic to the intrinsic is made by FT in its outlook upon observed variables. In more traditional statistical procedures, observed variables are typically regarded as important in their own right, the assumption being that given a problem domain, these particular variables are exactly the ones to be observed and analyzed. In FT, in contrast, the particular set of variables observed are looked upon as but a sample from a larger collection, possibly an infinite universe, of variables. Many subsets therefrom could have been observed for the same purpose. Hence, FT's concern with the sampling of variables to be observed and with techniques for making inferences from a sample of variables to the entire content universe.

Hypotheses of correspondence in FT are served by both the choice of definitional design and the choice of a data analytic procedure. In fact, FT seeks to establish a correspondence between an aspect of the definitional

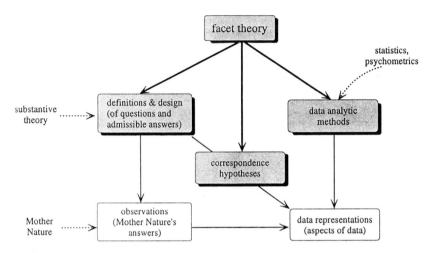

Figure 2.1. Schematic Overview of the Basic Elements of Facet Theory (FT), Their Relations to Each Other, and FT's Relation to Other Key Elements Involved in Empirical Research

system and an aspect of the observed data. Guttman (1982e) has emphasized that the search for such partnerships of definitions and data is the very purpose of scientific activity.

Finally, FT views scientific measurement not as any assignment of numbers to observed objects by some attribute but as an assignment of an *n*-tuple of scores, in which *n* is the smallest number commensurate with the "structure" of the attribute—that is, with its dimensionality and internal composition (see also Guttman, 1971). The foundations of *multiple scaling,* the technique for scientific measurement in this sense, have been laid by Shye (1985a).

Figure 2.1 shows diagrammatically how FT guides empirical research and theory construction in cooperation with two other key elements, substantive theory and Nature. FT and substantive theory both contribute to set up a definitional system for the universe of observations; that is, they clearly distinguish what one is going to investigate. This definitional system leads to a design for the concrete questions that one is going to pose to Nature. The answers to these questions—actually, a small portion of these answers—are the observations. The observations can be looked at with different means and using different perspectives. These include plots of marginal distributions, univariate statistics, contingency tables, and so forth, but also quite particular representations such as those produced by

SSA and other methods to be discussed later. The intention always is to study whether there are correspondences between design and observations.

Chapter 1 raised the question, for example, whether the facets could somehow correspond to the duration ratings. More concretely, it examined whether the mean ratings were ordered as predicted by the partial order of the structuples for the observations. Another question was whether the facets could be used to partition the four-dimensional SSA representation of the intercorrelations of the duration ratings into ordered regions. In both cases, it could be shown that the predictions were well confirmed.

FT as a Theory

In Guttman's early papers, FT was called *facet design and analysis*. He later changed his terminology to *facet theory*, but never gave an explicit reason for this change. It is unlikely, though, that this change was accidental, in that Guttman was always working on proper terminology (Borg, 1994). Indeed, he was willing—many felt too willing, causing confusion— to change his terminology if better terms seemed available. For example, he preferred to call MDS *smallest space analysis* or SSA, and later changed this to *similarity structure analysis*. Likewise he changed *multidimensional scalogram analysis* to *multidimensional structuple analysis* (Guttman, 1985c).

Why, then, facet *theory?* One answer can be given by considering what mathematicians call a theory: "the principles concerned with a certain concept, and the facts postulated and proved about it" (James & James, 1976, p. 387). FT is a theory in this sense, because it provides a system of concepts, definitions, and theorems on data analysis and mapping sentences.

Considering the definitions proposed by Guttman (1971) for measurement theory, statistical theory, and probability theory, such a formal perspective seems one possibility for Guttman's initial shift to facet theory. However, in 1973, Guttman (in Gratch, 1973) published yet another definition for theory, this time for the empirical sciences, which states that a theory is a "hypothesis of a correspondence between a definitional system for a universe of observations and an aspect of the empirical structure of those observations, together with a rationale for such an hypothesis" (p. 35). Guttman (1982e) later added about *rationale* that "An untested hypothesis should generally be accompanied by a rationale (not an 'explanation') to serve as a springboard for creating further partnerships for new laws should the hypothesis prove true, or for amending it should the hypothesis prove false" (Guttman, 1982e, p. 341). This definition of (scientific) theory was worked out after some years of incubation, but it was always implicit in Guttman's work in that he was always concerned with both sides of the empirical sciences, definitional systems, and data— in a "partnership."

In that FT does not suggest to construct observations on the basis of a faceted mapping sentence and to analyze them in particular ways without having something in mind, Guttman (1991) suggested that FT could also be considered a theory in this scientific sense. FT's main hypotheses can be formulated as follows:

> The higher the degree of formality of the mapping sentences used for designing the observations, the higher the reliability in constructing, making, and communicating observations.
>
> Designing a universe of observations in terms of explicit mapping sentences, and striving to enhance their level of formality, will, in the long run, be more successful for establishing scientific laws than using more implicit and intuitive definitional systems.

The first hypothesis seems immediately convincing. The more one makes sure that the definitions are clear for experts in the field and the more the instructions for data collection are made unambiguous, the more one should be able to eliminate imprecisions and errors. Reliability in this sense is, however, not sufficient for science. The real goal is, after all, to find empirical laws. And indeed, this is the field in which FT has its major advantages over less systematic approaches. There exist numerous publications in which FT has uncovered regularities that have not yet been seen in data previously published and analyzed with other methods (see, e.g., Borg & Staufenbiel, 1993; Guttman, 1965b; Guttman & Levy, 1991; Shye, 1978a, 1994a).

3 Observations

- Stimuli, Persons, and Responses
- Observations as Mappings

Stimuli, Persons, and Responses

In the social sciences, one is always concerned with three sets: P, the set of persons (i.e., subjects, informants, respondents or depending on the population studied, social groups, mice, rats, etc.) to whom certain questions are presented; Q, the set of questions (also experimental conditions, test stimuli, assessment situations, etc.); and R, the set of responses given by the persons (reactions, answers, ratings, judgments, etc.). Often, such sets that are of interest to us contain many but a finite number of elements. (Even the dense set *points in time* is divided in practice into a finite number of intervals.) In such cases, we may define a set by listing its elements. An example is the Likert scale $L =$ {very right, right, neither right nor wrong, wrong, very wrong}. Another example is the set of possible responses $R =$ {chicken, sirloin, omelette} to the question, What would you like to have for dinner? A third example is the set of questions of a questionnaire, $Q =$ {Question 1, Question 2, . . . , Question n}.

The usual notation for a set, that is, a sequential listing of its elements enclosed within braces, is often impractical for our purposes. Instead, we use *column* listings such as the following:

P Population	Q Questions	R Responses
(Person 1)	(Question 1)	(Response 1)
(Person 2)	(Question 2)	(Response 2)
.	.	.
(Person N)	(Question n)	(Response k)

The name of the facet is written on top of a column of elements that are held together by vertical arrays of parentheses.

Often we are interested in the population as a whole and do not distinguish a priori among observed persons. In such cases, the population facet may be denoted by (p) or $\{p\}$, in which p is a *place holder* for a typical element of the population facet.

As illustrated by the example of Chapter 1, the questions (stimuli) themselves can be broken down into one or more facets, each with any number of elements. In particular, a facet may have a single element in it—for example, goals = {money}. The braces here indicate that *money* is just one particular goal and others could be easily added but are left out at this time. Such a notation is used to make it clear that this is a facet that, although not studied further at the moment, may be worth considering in more detail in further research. A degenerate facet, such as goals = {money}, often offers a natural starting point for theory extensions.

Defining a facet by listing its elements is theoretically weak. It is better to formulate a rule by which one can decide whether a given element belongs to the facet. This is expressed as $A = \{a \mid$ list of properties of $a\}$. All things that possess all the properties listed after the | belong to A. The rule, consequently, is given by the properties of the set's elements, such as $P = \{p \mid p$ is a freshman at college C$\}$.

It is not always necessary to explicitly list a facet's properties. For example, with a facet such as population, it usually suffices to write (p), because the facet's name may be all one needs in order to know what elements are to replace the place holder p. Similarly, a facet such as gender is self-explanatory—that is, its elements are simply males and females.

It is important, on the other hand, to distinguish whether one deals with *samples* or *populations.* We sometimes distinguish them notationally by writing P, Q, and R for the respective samples, and **P** (population), **Q** (universe of questions), and **R** (universe of answers, range) for the respective universes from which the samples are drawn. Distinguishing samples and populations is commonplace when it comes to P but may seem peculiar at first for Q and for R. Yet a 5-point Likert scale is also a population—the universe of admissible answers for some question. What one actually observes may be just a subset of that universe. Then, the set Q of questions is, in practice, almost always but a small subset of the universe of possible questions of a particular type. This becomes clear by considering, for example, questions in an intelligence test or a questionnaire on political attitudes, in which thousands of questions could be asked.

Hence, in empirical research it must be clarified (a) by what criteria can one decide whether particular persons, questions, and responses, respectively, belong or do not belong to the domain of interest and (b) how the samples of persons, of questions, and of admissible responses should be drawn. Although the samples of persons and questions are drawn by the researcher, the sample of responses is usually drawn by Nature, so to speak: It is defined by the actual responses of the persons to the questions.

In the literature, one often finds the term *content universe* (Guttman, 1954c; Torgerson, 1958). Technically speaking, this sometimes denotes **Q**, and sometimes the set **Q** together with the answers that are admissible to the questions, **R**. Thus, in the first case, the content universe corresponds to the *universe of questions;* in the latter case, it means the *universe of items* that, in FT, always refers to the questions together with their ranges of admissible answers. Yet even though this is not always made explicit, the way in which the notion of content universe is used in context suggests that it is always meant to refer to items rather than just *questions,* because a question almost always *implies* what kind of answers are being sought. The difference between items and questions lies more in how explicit they are about their admissible range of answers.

Observations as Mappings

Mapping P × Q Into the Response Range R

The sets P, Q and R are linked to each other in the process of making observations. Assume, for example, that Q consists of the questions of a questionnaire, that, for reasons of simplicity, one asks all persons in P the same set of questions Q, and that each person p gives exactly one answer to each question. These observations constitute a mapping of the domain $P \times Q$ into the range R or, symbolically, $P \times Q \rightarrow R$. The set $P \times Q$ is the Cartesian product of the sets P and Q—that is, the set of all ordered pairs of elements of P and Q.

Consider an example. We conduct a small survey, asking n persons in the street,

$$\frac{P}{}$$

(p_1 = Person 1)
(p_2 = Person 2)

.
.

(p_n = Person n),

the following questions:

Q
(q_1 = Are you interested in politics?)
(q_2 = Which political party do you prefer?)
(q_3 = Do you read the *Times* every day?).

This renders as the Cartesian product, P × Q:

P × Q		P × Q	
((p_1,q_1))		((Person p_1, Are you interested in politics?)	)
((p_1,q_2))	=	((Person p_1, Which political party do you prefer?)	)
((p_1,q_3))		((Person p_1, Do you read the *Times* every day?)	)
((p_2,q_1))		((Person p_2, Are you interested in politics?)	)
.		.	
((p_n,q_3))		((Person p_n, Do you read the *Times* every day?)	)

The elements of P × Q are ordered pairs, written as (p,q), in which p is an element of P and q is an element of Q. This can also be represented as

	q_1	q_2	q_3
p_1	(p_1,q_1)	(p_1,q_2)	(p_1,q_3)
p_2	(p_2, q_1)	(p_2, q_2)	(p_2, q_3)
.	.	.	.
p_n	(p_n, q_1)	(p_n, q_2)	(p_n, q_3)

The table better shows the meaning of the "cross" in P × Q, because here we actually see how the persons are crossed with the questions.

Assume now that we defined—by design of the questionnaire format—the following responses as admissible ones:

R
(r_1 = Yes)
(r_2 = No)
(r_3 = Democrats)
(r_4 = Republicans)
(r_5 = Other)
(r_6 = Don't Know)

Whatever other behavior the persons exhibit as a response to the questions $q_1, \ldots, q_3$—as in asking for clarification or scratching their scalps—is of no interest to us, or in any case will not be recorded. The observations consist in assigning exactly one element of R to each element of P × Q. This assignment is actually done by the responding person through his or her answers. Formally, this yields a mapping of P × Q to R, because every element of the domain P × Q is linked to exactly one element of the range R.

Such mappings can be represented differently. One possibility is a simple listing with arrows as follows:

$$
\begin{array}{rcl}
(\ p_1, q_1\ ) & \rightarrow & r_1 \\
(\ p_1, q_2\ ) & \rightarrow & r_4 \\
(\ p_1, q_3\ ) & \rightarrow & r_2 \\
(\ p_2, q_1\ ) & \rightarrow & r_1 \\
& \cdot & \\
(\ p_n, q_3\ ) & \rightarrow & r_2.
\end{array}
$$

Formally equivalent but less "dynamic" is to represent the mapping by the set of 3-tuples: $\{(p_1, q_1, r_1), (p_1, q_2, r_4), (p_1, q_3, r_2), (p_2, q_1, r_1), \ldots, (p_n, q_3, r_2)\}$. Another possibility is to use an *incidence matrix:*

	r_1	r_2	r_3	r_4	r_5	r_6
(p_1, q_1)	1	0	0	0	0	0
(p_1, q_2)	0	0	0	1	0	0
(p_1, q_3)	0	1	0	0	0	0
(p_2, q_1)	1	0	0	0	0	0
$\cdot$	$\cdot$	$\cdot$	$\cdot$	$\cdot$	$\cdot$	$\cdot$
(p_n, q_3)	0	1	0	0	0	0

Each row in this matrix contains exactly one 1. It denotes the answer that the particular person gave to the particular question. A 0 stands for "that particular answer was not observed."

Assume now that some person says, for example, that she prefers both the Democrats and the Republicans equally over others, or assume no answer is recorded for some persons (missing data). Such cases would lead to incidence matrices that do not represent mappings of P × Q into R, because in a mapping, each element of the domain must be related to exactly one element of the range. We can, however, preserve the unifying mapping notion for observations if we replace R by its power set 2^R. The elements of 2^R are all subsets of R and, therefore, *any* combination of R's elements. The set 2^R also contains the empty set (no answer) as one of its elements.

Finally, we may also think of Q (or P) as a set of operators that map the elements of P (or Q, respectively) onto elements of R or of 2^R. That is, the questions map the persons into the elements of the range, or, alternatively, the persons map the questions into the range.

Mapping P × Q Into an Indexed Range

The above design is not yet satisfactory because it suggests, for example, that r_3 (Democrats) is an acceptable answer to q_1 (Are you interested in politics?). So let us now refine our notation and link it to the more usual one. We begin by indexing the elements of R with the questions q_1, q_2, ..., q_n. Thus, $r_i(q_j)$ is the i-th admissible answer to question q_j. This produces the following:

Rq
($r_1(q_1)$ = Yes)
($r_2(q_1)$ = No)
($r_3(q_1)$ = Don't Know)
($r_1(q_2)$ = Democrats)
($r_2(q_2)$ = Republicans)
($r_3(q_2)$ = Other)
($r_4(q_2)$ = Don't Know)
($r_1(q_3)$ = Yes)
($r_2(q_3)$ = No)
($r_3(q_3)$ = Don't Know)

The *Yes* from the range R appears twice as a possible answer to q_1 and to q_3. These cases are, however, well distinguished by the indexing of the answers in R. We thus write P × Q → Rq and obtain the following tabular representation:

	$r_1(q_1)$	$r_2(q_1)$	$r_3(q_1)$	$r_1(q_2)$	...	$r_4(q_2)$	...	$r_2(q_3)$	$r_3(q_3)$
(p_1, q_1)	1	0	0	0	.	0	.	0	0
(p_1, q_2)	0	0	0	0	.	1	.	0	0
(p_1, q_3)	0	0	0	0	.	0	.	1	0
(p_2, q_1)	1	0	0	0	.	0	.	0	0
.	.	.	.	.	.	.	.	.	.
(p_n, q_3)	0	0	0	0	.	0	.	1	0

In this table, we shaded those cells in gray in which a 1 can in principle appear. Person p_1 can only answer question q_1 with one of the response categories for q_1—that is, with either $r_1(q_1)$, $r_2(q_1)$, or $r_3(q_1)$, but not, for example, $r_1(q_2)$. The white cells, therefore, are automatically filled with zeroes. Moreover, in that there can only be one 1 per row, we can reduce the number of columns to three. We achieve this by using i in $r_i(q_j)$ as a cell entry in a column indexed with q_j. This yields the usual persons-by-variables data matrix:

	p_1	q_2	q_3
p_1	1	4	1
p_2	1	.	.
.	.	.	.
p_n	.	.	2

Mapping Persons by Questions Into Data Structuples

Rather than using indexing on the answers, we can bring out the same distinctions in a simpler and more natural way by writing the range as a Cartesian product, $R^q = R(q_1) \times R(q_2) \times R(q_3)$: that is, explicitly, by writing

$$R^q = \begin{array}{l} \underline{\quad R(q_1) \quad} \\ (\ r_1(q_1) = \text{Yes} \\ (\ r_2(q_1) = \text{No} \\ (\ r_3(q_1) = \text{Don't Know} \end{array} \begin{array}{l} \\ ) \\ ) \times \\ ) \end{array} \begin{array}{l} \underline{\quad R(q_2) \quad} \\ (\ r_2(q_2) = \text{Democrats} \\ (\ r_3(q_2) = \text{Republicans} \\ (\ r_4(q_2) = \text{Other} \\ (\ r_5(q_2) = \text{Don't Know} \end{array} \begin{array}{l} \\ ) \\ ) \times \\ ) \\ ) \end{array} \begin{array}{l} \underline{\quad R(q_3) \quad} \\ (\ r_1(q_3) = \text{Yes}\ ) \\ (\ r_2(q_3) = \text{No}\ ), \end{array}$$

in which each *range facet*, $R(q_i)$, is indexed by the question q_i whose admissible answers it provides. Each person, then, is mapped by each particular question, q_i, into a particular range, $R(q_i)$. If we want to express the entire empirical inquiry as one mapping, then a proper way to formulate it is to say that the set of questions, Q, operates on the set of persons, P, so that each element of P is mapped into an element of R^q, $Q(P) \rightarrow R^q$. The elements of R^q are called *data structuples* (data profiles). To formally take care of the possibility of "missing data," each $R(q_i)$ could be extended by adding the element *no answer*.

4 Definitional Systems

- Facets as Sets
- Relations and Facets
- Facetizations
- Definitional Shifts Between Content Facets and Range Facets

Facets as Sets

The building blocks of FT are facets. A facet is a set of elements (i.e., types, classes, categories, attributes, etc.) that classify objects of interest. Facets make distinctions that are, by definition or by hypothesis, relevant for the scientific investigation. The facet *gender,* for example, partitions a population of persons into two subsets, males and females. The facet *intelligence level* splits the same population into a set of ordered classes ranging from *very intelligent* to *very stupid.* Intelligence test items—such as arithmetical, geometrical, and verbal—can be classified by the facet *kind of test material.* Responses to attitudinal items can be classified by a scale ranging from *very positive* to *very negative* behavior toward the object of concern.

Relations and Facets

Relations

We now briefly define a number of notions that are useful for characterizing the roles of facets in theory construction.

Every subset $\mathfrak{R}$ of the Cartesian product $M \times M$ is called a *binary relation* on M. Relations characterize how the elements of M are linked to each other. As an example, consider the relation $\mathfrak{R}$ = "likes" on the set P = {Linda, Hans, Mike}. The Cartesian product is P × P = {(Linda, Linda), (Linda, Hans), . . . , (Mike, Mike)}. $\mathfrak{R}$, then, specifies the pairs (i,j) for which the relation "i likes j" holds. This is best shown in a relation matrix, in which a 1 shows that row element i is $\mathfrak{R}$-related to column element j:

	Linda	Hans	Mike
Linda	1	1	0
Hans	0	0	1
Mike	1	1	1

Instead of stating that "the pair (i,j) is an element of $\mathfrak{R}$," one can simply write "$i\mathfrak{R}j$" for binary relations, just as one says that "x likes y" in ordinary language or $x = y$ in mathematics.

Properties of Relations

Some properties of relations play such an important role that they have been given special names. Thus, a relation that contains all elements in the main diagonal of its relation matrix is called *reflexive*. Obviously, then, the "likes" relation as specified in the matrix above is not reflexive, because Hans does not like himself. A relation is *symmetric* if, whenever $i\mathfrak{R}j$, then also $j\mathfrak{R}i$. This property also does not hold in the above example, because Linda likes Hans, but Hans does not like Linda. A relation is *transitive* if $i\mathfrak{R}k$ is true whenever both $i\mathfrak{R}j$ and $j\mathfrak{R}k$ hold. This property is also not fulfilled in the above example, in that Linda likes Hans, Hans likes Mike, but Linda does not like Mike.

A relation that is reflexive, symmetric, and transitive is called an *equivalence relation*. One example for an equivalence relation is the relation = for numbers, because it holds that $x = x$; if $x = y$, then $y = x$; and if $x = y$ and $y = z$, then $x = z$ also, for any numbers x, y, z. The *relation matrix* of an equivalence relation has a block structure or, in any case, can always be permuted into a block structure. Let $M = \{a,b,c,d,e,f\}$; then the following relation matrix defines an equivalence relation (=), in which $a = b$, $b = a$, $c = d$, $d = c$, . . . , $a = a$, . . . , $f = f$.

	a	b	c	d	e	f
a	1	1	0	0	0	0
b	1	1	0	0	0	0
c	0	0	1	1	1	0
d	0	0	1	1	1	0
e	0	0	1	1	1	0
f	0	0	0	0	0	1

Another important class of relations is *order relations* or simply *orders.* Its prototype is the *weak* order $\geq$ (is greater than or equal to) for numbers. The relation $\geq$ is obviously reflexive and transitive. Moreover, $\geq$ is also *antisymmetric;* that is, if $x \geq y$ and $y \geq x$, then $x = y$. If, for a given set, $\geq$ is also *complete* (i.e., if $x\mathcal{R}y$ or $y\mathcal{R}x$ for any $x \neq y$), then the set is *ordered.* In a *partly ordered* set, in contrast, there may be pairs of elements, say x,y for which neither $x \geq y$ nor $y \geq x$. In such a case we say that x and y are *incomparable.*

In the social sciences, many variants of orders are used (Roberts, 1979). One further example is the *strong,* linear order, with > (greater than) for numbers as an illustration. In that all orders have one property in common, transitivity, Coombs, Dawes, and Tversky (1970, p.368) speak of *order* whenever a relation is transitive.

Partitions

A *partition* of a set M is a set of subsets (*equivalence classes*) of M such that each element of M is in exactly one subset of M. Thus, the subsets are disjoint and exhaustive of M. For example, if $M = \{a,b,c,d,e,f\}$, then $\mathcal{P} = \{\{a,b\},\{c,d,e\},\{f\}\}$ is a partition of M. This is illustrated in the following diagram.

f	c	a
	d	b
	e	

It is important to distinguish between the partition—a set whose elements are classes of points—and the partitioned set whose elements are "points." In the first case, the elements of each class, when mapped into the class, lose their individual properties except those that define the class. In a sense, partitioning a set corresponds to a process of reducing and abstracting individual cases to "types." Real numbers, for example, are reduced to even and odd numbers, eggs are sorted into small, medium, and large ones, and respondents are classified as males and females. Partitioning intelligence test items into verbal, numerical, and geometrical types is yet another example.

The elements of each class are all equal in a sense. Every time one is filing, sorting, or classifying objects, one is in fact partitioning a set. Hence, each equivalence relation on M partitions M, and, conversely, a partition on M defines an equivalence relation on M. Every pair of elements pertaining to the same class are equal. For example, in the previous partition, $a\mathscr{C}b$ and $c\mathscr{C}d$, in which $\mathscr{C}$ denotes the equivalence relation induced by the given partition.

Facets and Relations

The sense in which the elements of the classes {a,b}, {c,d,e} and {f} in the previous diagram are equivalent cannot be derived from the Venn diagram above. In contrast, the substantive meaning of a facet like gender needs no further explanation. This facet represents a substantive *rule* for deciding whether a person belongs to the class male or female. With this facet, any set of persons can be partitioned. We say that two persons are equivalent if they belong to the same class.

What we observe here is true for facets in general. In that every facet partitions the set of interest in terms of substantively meaningful rules, it defines an equivalence relation on that set. The relation may have additional properties: for example, it may partition the set into ordered classes as in an order of the $\geq$ variety.

Facets and Systems

A set with a relation defined on it is called a *system* or a *structured set*. It is written as $<M, \mathscr{R}>$, in which M is a set and $\mathscr{R}$ a relation on M. The relation $\mathscr{R}$, in turn, is induced by some facet F, which we denote by $\mathscr{R}(F)$. For example, the facet gender structures P, the population of persons, and turns it into the system $<P, \mathscr{R}(\text{gender})>$, a quotient set of P.

Consider now the case in which we have n relations on M, $\mathscr{R}_1, \ldots, \mathscr{R}_n$. The conjunction of all n relations on M is defined as the intersection $\mathscr{R}$ of $\mathscr{R}_1, \ldots, \mathscr{R}_n$. That is, $i\mathscr{R}j$ is the subset of $M \times M$ that satisfies all relations.

Substantively, $\mathfrak{R}$ can be traced back to the Cartesian product of the facets $F_1 \times \ldots \times F_n$, in which F_i is the facet that defines $\mathfrak{R}i$.

As an example, let M be the set of citizens of Seattle. Let the facet associated with $\mathfrak{R}_1$ be gender. For $\mathfrak{R}_2$, the relevant facet may be city district = {Downtown, East, . . . ,}. $\mathfrak{R}_1$ and $\mathfrak{R}_2$ are both equivalence relations. Together, they sort the citizens of Seattle by two criteria into a set of classes. These classes correspond to the elements of the facet product G × D, which consists of the pairs (male, Downtown), (female, Downtown), (male, East), and so forth.

Facetizations

Facetizations of P

We now consider how a system is generated and what roles facets play in this process. Sociologists, in particular, are used to spending time and effort in structuring the population P by various person facets, $P_1, \ldots, P_n$. Assume we want to conduct a survey. The population is defined as all citizens (of some country) who are entitled to vote. We can symbolically represent this population as

Citizens Entitled to Vote

Rarely is such an unstructured population of much use in practical research. Moreover, for sampling considerations, one usually wants to ensure that any sample from this population contains both men and women. Consequently, one stratifies the population by the facet {male, female}, which leads to the following partitioning of P:

Male Citizens Entitled to Vote
Female Citizens Entitled to Vote

Even that may be too coarse for some purposes. Hence, assume we also decide to consider *age* as an additional facet, and specify it as { 18-30 years

old, 31-50 years old, 51-65 years old, older than 65}. This leads to a
cross-facetization of P as follows:

(M,18-30)	(M,31-50)	(M,51-65)	(M,>65)
(F,18-30)	(F,31-50)	(F,51-65)	(F,>65)

in which $(M,18\text{-}30)$ = male citizens aged 18-30 who are entitled to vote
and $(F,>65)$ = female citizens over 65 years old who are entitled to vote.
The eight-cell table is the Cartesian product of the facets gender = $\{M,F\}$
and A = age = $\{18\text{-}30, 31\text{-}50, 51\text{-}65, >65\}$. At the same time, it also
represents the set of equivalence classes (*quotient set*) that $G \times A$ induces
in P. We denote this set by $P/G \times A$. Each class in $P/G \times A$ is characterized
by the pair (g,a), in which g belongs to G and a belongs to A. Less formally,
what we have are person *types*, each one typified by a particular combination of gender and age. We could also say that G and A generate the system
$<P, \Re(G \times A)>$, in which $\Re(G \times A)$ is the equivalence relation induced by
$G \times A$.

We could continue with this example and add further facets to structure
P. With a third facet, we would obtain a three-dimensional table of cells,
one for each type. With further facets, such tables become impractical.
Listings of structuples are better. For example,

{ $(M,$ 18-30, less than 1000 $ net income, California, . . .),
    $(F,$ 18-30, less than 1000 $ net income, California, . . .), . . . },

or, in compact form, $P/\Re(\text{Gender} \times \text{Age} \times \text{Net Income} \times \text{State}) = \{$person
type $(g,a,i,s, \ldots)$ | g is an element of $\{M,F\}$, a is an age group . . .}.

Facetizations of Q

In addition to P, one can also facetize Q, the set of stimuli or questions. In
the social sciences, such facetizations are usually made implicitly rather than
explicitly. Often, the questions in an empirical study are more or less unsys-
tematic collections or "pools" of items that possess some vague substantive
commonality like "intelligence" or "attitude toward religion."

An exception in this regard is Guilford's (1967) structure of intellect
model, which is a facetization of intelligence test items, or a "three-way

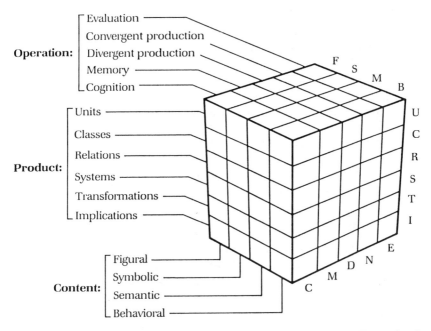

Figure 4.1. Guilford's (1967) Structure of Intelligence Model as an Example of Facetizing Q

SOURCE: Reprinted with permission from *The structure and measurement of intelligence,* H. J. Eysenck, 1979, New York: Springer-Verlag.

organization of intellectual tasks" (Cronbach, 1971, p. 263). Figure 4.1 shows that Guilford structures the set of intelligence test items in a three-fold way: (a) by the operation that the tasks require, (b) by the products that the candidate is supposed to deliver, and (c) by the content of the tasks. "Each combination represents a type of task which is or can be represented in an intellectual task" (Cronbach, 1971, p. 263).

In the experimental sciences, such facetizations are commonplace. If an experiment is planned, then the researcher usually pays particular attention to the facets of Q. The facets are called (experimental) factors. Formally, Q is being facetized into $Q/Q_1 \times Q_2 \times \ldots \times Q_n$. The facets Q_i ($i = 1, \ldots, n$) are called content facets. A simple example is an experimental design for the dependency of some performance measure of P = Rats on Q = Drive × Habit × Incentive = {0, 1, 2 hours of deprivation of food} × {0, 10, 20 previous trials in runway} × {0, 1, 2, 3 food pellets in last trial}.

Facetizations and Universes

The close relationship of facets and universes can lead to conceptual ambiguities. Consider the following lines from Dancer (1990a):

> A principal idea underlying facet theory is that in virtually all empirical investigations in the social sciences, the particular collection of variables used . . . are selected not because of an interest the investigator holds in these specific variables, but more likely because they are thought to be representative of some larger . . . universe. (p. 367)

This is indeed true, and, moreover, a fundamental premise of FT. Dancer states further that,

> defining this universe in terms of sets that depict its various fundamental conceptual (semantic) characteristics, is fundamental to set theory. . . . The collection of all such facets can be used to formulate a definition of the construct because, presumably, each facet reflects an essential component of a content universe of variables that depict the construct. (p. 367)

This can be misleading in that the role of facets is generally not to *define* a universe, but rather to *structure* a given unstructured universe.

Taking a closer look at many item definitions, one would find, however, that domain facets often implicitly restrict the universe of items. This is almost always the case if there are domain facets that do not contain elements such as "in general" or "unspecified," because such facets are often not exhaustive. Therefore, all items that do not satisfy one of the elements explicated in any such facet are automatically excluded from the universe of items (see also Chapter 7, Intelligence Items).

Items are defined by their questions (elements of Q) and their response ranges (R). If one thinks about the behavior that one wants to study, then R is of primary interest. Ideally, it is true that only after one has decided what R one wants to study, it becomes interesting to consider different conditions under which this should be done. For this reason, generally, it is R that defines what the items have in common, whereas facetizing Q specifies differences among them. Guilford's intelligence cube obviously does not define intelligence items but distinguishes among different types of intelligence items.

Facets of Q can be used, in any case, to filter out subsets from a given universe that are of particular interest. For example, one may want to look at the universe of simple tasks of addition such as $2 + 2 = ?$, which form a subset of the universe of intelligence test items. Such restrictions of items to particular types require, of course, that the universe be defined beforehand.

In defining such universes, even the experimental sciences sometimes proceed in a rather undisciplined fashion. They are usually quite explicit in their facetizations of *Q*, but what one should take as the universe of items often requires interpretation. Consequently, the *universe of discourse* is also left undefined. As a typical example, consider the above designs on the performance of rats in mazes. Are they really meant to capture learning or even principles of behavior (Hull, 1943)? Clearly, they study appetitive behavior of rats toward water and food in a maze. Yet to what extent and how could the observations made in this context be generalized? This is difficult to say, as long as it is not made clear along which lines such generalizations should be made. Possible answers to this question are actually not so difficult: They can be derived from explicating and extending the facets of the observations. First, an obvious facet that offers itself for generalization is the degenerate facet *maze,* but *rats* and *food/water* also could be substituted by broader content classes that include other respondents and other reinforcers, respectively.

Factorial Surveys

For questionnaire construction, facetizations mostly have been used more implicitly than explicitly. A remarkable exception in this regard is the "factorial survey approach" (Rossi & Nock, 1982). It uses particular "vignettes" as objects for the respondents' judgments. These vignettes are bundles of short descriptions for the elements of the different facets of the design.

As an example, Rossi & Anderson (1982) studied the facets ("dimensions") of judgments on sexual harassment. In one particular study, they looked at eight facets: (a) *status of male* = {single graduate student, single graduate student TA, married graduate student, . . . , married 65-year-old professor}; (b) *status of female* = {single graduate student, freshman, senior, married graduate student}; (c) *woman's relationship to man* = {had rarely had occasion to talk to, had gone out several times with, . . . }; (d) *social setting;* (e) *woman's receptivity;* (f) *male's verbal behavior;* (g) *male's physical acts;* and (h) *male's threat.*

The set of all combinations (structuples) of levels of the facets is termed *factorial object universe.* A vignette is an "object—a unit being judged that is described in terms of a single level for every dimension" (Rossi & Anderson, 1982, p. 28). Hence, such vignettes can be simply listed by a computer program and require no further substantive thoughts. This yields, for example, the following:

Cindy M., a married graduate student; often had occasion to talk to; Gary T., a single 65-year-old professor; they were both at a party; she said that she enjoyed and looked forward to his class; he asked her about her other courses; he said that she could substantially improve her grade if she cooperated.

"Cindy M." and "Gary T." are irrelevant constants that are meant to make the vignettes more readable.

The respondents were asked to rate such vignettes on a 9-point scale ranging from *definitely not harassment* to *definitely harassment*. Rossi and Anderson (1982) analyzed the resulting data by regression:

> Each of the levels that define the factorial object set has been expressed as binary (dummy) variables and used as independent variables in the ordinary least squares regression [additive model without interaction terms, IB & SS] of the judgments made on factorial object characteristics . . . The resulting regression coefficients . . . express the extent to which judgments are affected by the presence of a particular level in a factorial object that is being rated. (p. 44)

Obtrusive and Unobtrusive Facetizations

The above vignettes led to items in which the facets are quite obtrusive. Actually, vignettes are essentially nothing but structuples. Thus, they have the advantage that they can be easily generated (e.g., by a simple computer program). Yet this transparency may also be a disadvantage at times. In experiments, in particular, one typically wants stimulus conditions that are not so transparent to the subjects. This is often true for questionnaires as well. Moreover, posing one's questions in forms of vignettes may sometimes produce stimuli that are long and difficult to understand.

In contrast, consider a question asked by Levy (1976): "How satisfied are you with your present job?" Unlike a vignette, this question is phrased in natural language that is easy to understand. Levy (1976) defines the content of this question by $a1b1$, in which $a1$ means *work* in the facet $A =$ life area, and $b1$ means *primary environment* in the facet $B =$ environment of person. The element $a1$ is quite obtrusively put forward in the question, whereas it should not be obvious that the question relates to the respondent's primary environment.

An even more unobtrusive facetization is exemplified by Levy and Guttman (1975) in the following question. They characterize the question "How is your mood these days?" through five facets as $a1b1c2d1e8$ or, expressed verbally, as "satisfied to be with respect to some unspecified condition of one's primary environment in life area unspecified," in which $a1$ = satisfied, $b1$ = be, and so forth. Clearly, what we have here is a question whose content is a construction of the researcher that remains largely hidden from the respondent. The question is also easy to understand and easy to answer. On the other hand, given the facet system on which the structuple is based, different researchers are more likely to disagree on exactly which structuple should be assigned to this question. For vignettes, this is not an issue.

Explicit and Implicit Facetizations

Novices at FT often agree that design is useful and possibly even necessary, but that their particular problems are far too complex for such a seemingly simplistic approach as FT. A theoretical discussion of such matters usually leads nowhere until one finally looks at the questions the researcher seeks to pose and the responses he or she seeks to collect. Studying these items typically allows one to identify quite easily the "distractors" the researcher has built into his or her questions. This is often the beginning of systematic efforts at designing the research question in a more explicit way.

Consider a classic example from Bastide and van den Berghe (1957) in which they distinguished four types of attitudes toward social behaviors of Whites vis-à-vis Blacks. According to Guttman (1959b), these types can be described in abstract form as follows:

1. *Stereotype:* Belief of a White subject that his own group {does, does not} excel in comparison with Blacks on desirable traits.
2. *Norm:* Belief of a White subject that his own group {ought, ought not} interact with Blacks in social ways.
3. *Hypothetical Interaction:* Belief of a White subject that he himself {will, will not} interact with Blacks in social ways.
4. *Personal Interaction:* Overt action of a White subject himself {to, not to} interact with Blacks in social ways. (p. 319)

By studying these classes of behavior more closely and looking for features that vary systematically, one notes that the first three begin with *belief* and the last one with *overt action*. This source of conceptual variance constitutes a facet, *A,* that could be called "modality of attitude toward social behavior" with elements belief and overt action. Formally, $A = \{a_1$ = belief, a_2 = overt action}. Two further facets are also obvious. They make distinctions regarding the attitude object: B = reference group = { b_1 = Whites in general, b_2 = respondent him/herself} and C = relation of reference group to Blacks = {c_1 = compare, c_2 = interact}.

The behavior classes, therefore, follow a rule of formation that can be expressed as follows: A white person assesses, in a particular modality (A), the attitudinal behavior of the reference group (B) relating to Blacks in terms of (C). With the distinctions they make, the three facets imply $2 \times 2 \times 2 = 8$ types of attitudinal behavior. Each one of them is characterized by a structuple like $a_1b_1c_1$ or $a_2b_2c_1$. Four of these behavior types correspond to what was described by Bastide and van den Berghe (1957):

Behavior	Structuple
1. Stereotype	$a_1b_1c_1$
2. Norm	$a_1b_1c_2$
3. Hypothetical interaction	$a_1b_2c_2$
4. Personal interaction	$a_2b_2c_2$

The four remaining structuples also make sense substantively. We show them together with labels (Guttman, 1959b) that are meant to capture their content.

Behavior	Structuple
5. Feel superior	$a_1b_2c_1$
6. Act superior	$a_2b_2c_1$
7. Teach	$a_2b_1c_1$
8. Preach	$a_2b_1c_2$

It could be asked why Bastide and van den Berghe did not also refer to these classes of behavior. After all, they proposed a system of attitudes that implicitly contains the three facets described above. As an answer, one can only guess that their intuitive approach made it difficult for them to actually see all the classes their distinctions imply.

Explicating the facets allows one to see, moreover, that the elements in each content facet are ordered from *weak* to *strong* social behavior of Whites vis-à-vis Blacks, because each facet is ordered in the sense of weak-to-strong social behavior. For example, actual social interactions of Whites with Blacks are, as "overt actions," stronger than mere "beliefs" in such interactions. Similar arguments hold for Facets B and C, so that for each facet in turn, elements indexed by the number 2 indicate stronger social behavior than elements denoted by 1. This implies a partial order on the content structuples (Figure 4.2), in which *action* attributed to *self* with respect to social *interaction* $(a_2b_2c_2)$ is the strongest type of attitudinal behavior and *belief* attributed to one's *group* with respect to *comparisons* $(a_1b_1c_1)$ is the weakest type.

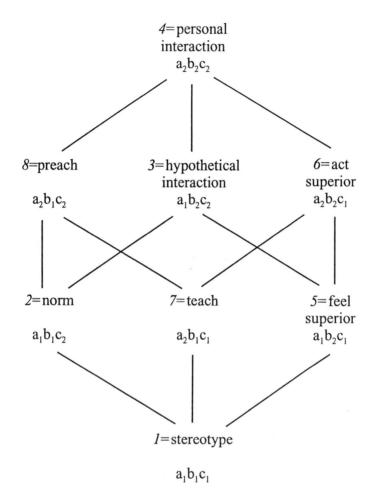

Figure 4.2. Partial Order of Behavior Structuples

So we see that using a simple technique for explicating what was formulated in a more intuitive way allows one to see the complete universe of behavior types implied by the three distinctions, and also its structure, a partial order. Moreover, the partial order scalogram procedures commonly applied to data structuples (see Chapter 10) are, in principle, applicable here too. Indeed, Guttman applied partial-order analysis to analyze projective techniques classified in terms of content structuples

(Guttman, 1972), and structuples that distinguish among different varieties of social groups (Guttman, 1982e).

The partial order defined on the content structuples may serve as a rationale for a hypothesis about the observations: For the intercorrelations of behavior Types 1, 2, 3 and 4 that are reported by Bastide and van den Berghe (1957), a simplex gradient can be expected. Indeed, behavior types that appeared closer on the cumulative conceptual scale 1-4—such as stereotype and norm—correlated more positively in general than more distant behavior types—such as stereotype and hypothetical interaction (see Figure 4.2).

Finding and Defining Facets

How can one find good facets? Unfortunately, there is no mechanical procedure. Rather, "the initial choice of facets depends on the creativity and perceptiveness of the theorist" (Wiggins, 1980, p. 477). Facets, once formulated, are not permanently fixed. This is true even in physics. If there are alternatives that are clearer in their semantics, simpler to use, associated with fewer exceptions, or better suited for constructing a particular theory, then such definitions will be adopted. "Time is defined so that motion looks simple" (Misher, Thorne, & Wheeler as cited in Guttman, 1991, p. 61). *Simple* here means that this particular definition of time simplifies relativity theory. For other purposes, this definition of time may be quite useless—for example, defining the length of a pause in the military. For this, *one cigarette* may provide the better, more pertinent, measurement.

Facets usually also have a history. At first, one is satisfied if they are reasonably clear and if they are mirrored in the data at all. Better predictions can usually be achieved by introducing further controlling facets, but typically the initial facets have to be modified more or less in an interplay ("partnership," according to Guttman, 1991) between conceptual work and empirical testing. Modifications also become necessary if the facets are semantically blurred so that different experts cannot agree on what they mean and, thus, arrive at different structuple assignments.

Structuple Assignments: Assumptions or Definitions?

It is not always easy to code items within a system of facets, that is, to assign them to structuples. Elizur (1984), for example, classifies the work value "advancement in one's job" as a "cognitive" value relative to the facet {cognitive, affective, instrumental} values. One could ask why advancement was not coded as affective or as instrumental. After all, advancement typically should be a pleasant event and also be related to a higher salary. Thus, is Elizur's assignment of the struct cognitive correct? This question turns out to be meaningless, because structuple assignments are definitional *specifications*. If they were hypotheses, one could check or would indeed be interested to check whether they are true. For definitions, on the other hand, such a test is obviously impossible. Definitions are not true or false. Rather, other goodness criteria are relevant, in particular their semantic clarity and their usefulness for theory construction. Structuple assignments, just like hypotheses, however, are typically not accidental either but rather are suggested by empirical facts and reasoning.

The clarity of the structuple assignment partially reflects the clarity of the facets on which they are based. Ideally, different experts should be able to work reliably with the facets so that they arrive at identical classifications for given objects. If that is so, then the facets are at least conceptually useful because they guarantee some *conceptual control* over the given universe of discourse. The ultimate question, of course, is whether the facets also provide *empirical control*—that is, whether the structuples can be used to structure and organize the observations or, expressed differently, whether they contribute to theory.

Elizur's (1984) struct assignments for work values are useful primarily in the empirical sense. Their semantic clarity, on the other hand, is limited. This is not so much a consequence of the vagueness of the distinctions made by the facet {cognitive, affective, instrumental}, but rather due to the undifferentiated nature of advancement that, in one way or another, relates to all these outcomes. One could argue, though, that, for the studied population, the cognitive aspects of advancement dominate affective and instrumental aspects. This could be the case if by advancement people primarily think of more interesting work.

A lack of clarity between definitions and hypotheses usually surfaces somewhere else: Semantic classifications are often confused with statistical discriminability or correlation. Statistical properties, however, have no implication for content whatsoever, even though it is common practice in "item analysis" to eliminate an item from an item pool simply because it does not correlate highly with the other items, or leave an item in this pool for just the opposite reason. It is easy to see that this practice is unfounded, because it cannot be tested if a structuple assignment is true. Even two items that correlate with $r = 1$ need not measure the same thing. To do that, the two items must also share the same meaning in their ranges, which is a semantic criterion. In themselves, correlations allow no inference on the content of the variables but only indicate how two variables covary empirically.

Mixing up semantic-logical and statistical-empirical (in)dependence is often due to premature interests in applications or an "engineering" perspective (Coombs, personal communication, 1978). If one can reliably predict x from knowing y, then it is indeed uneconomical to measure both x and y. But a high correlation on which this prediction is based may vanish under certain conditions. For example, it seems reasonable to hypothesize that the positive correlation that is found between knowledge in biology and in literature among high school students would decline considerably (or even vanish) among literary critics.

These considerations are, however, of limited use when it comes to assigning structuples to items. For that purpose, it is often useful in practice to take the facets in an "as if" sense. That is, one puts oneself into the subject's shoes and speculates whether the subject's response is based on the same distinctions that the facets formulate.

This leads to the question whether setting up a system of facets actually means that one is formulating hypotheses about the subject's cognitive structure or, more bluntly, about how the subject thinks. Fischer (1990) accordingly argued that structuple assignments are not definitions but "guesses." Although we refer to some subtle points here, we find it simpler to think of structuple assignments as definitions and of their correspondence to observations as hypotheses.

Multiple Structuple Assignments

It is a question of major practical importance of what should be done in case structuple assignments cannot be agreed upon. Consider an example. Jurgensen (1978) asked respondents how important it is for them "to have work that is interesting and that they like." Elizur (1984) codes this item as a question about a cognitive work reward content. One can argue, however, that the *like* makes this item more emotional than cognitive. Such ambiguities are typical for the case in which one wants to sort given items into a facet system designed afterward.

If one constructs items from scratch, one can and must avoid such cases of ambiguity. Thus, Borg and Galinat (1986) split the Jurgensen item into two items: One asked for the importance of having an interesting job; the other one assessed the importance of having work that is fun. Ambiguity, in addition, can be reduced by making implicit facets explicit, thus "cleaning" the items from implicit but irrelevant semantic noise.

But what can be done with a given item whose meaning remains ambiguous? Consider again the case of the work value advancement, which is seen by different theories and researchers either as an affective, as a cognitive, or as an instrumental value. If one cannot split this item into three more homogenous items and collect data for them separately, one can split the trichotomous facet {affective, cognitive, instrumental} into three dichotomous facets:

Modality	Affective Modality	Cognitive Modality	Instrumental Modality
(Affective)	(Affective)	(Cognitive)	(Instrumental)
(Cognitive) → (	( )	( )	( )
(Instrumental)	(Not Affective)	(Not Cognitive)	(Not Instrumental)

With these three modality facets it is easy to classify an item whose content seems ambiguous. One now has, for example, affective-cognitive, cognitive-instrumental, or affective-instrumental work values.

Resolving a single qualitative facet into a battery of such dummy facets may seem a cheap way out of necessary conceptual work. But when questions carry complex shades of meanings, employing dummy facets as content facets may be a necessary analytic procedure (see also Schlesinger, 1978).

Modifying Structuples

It sometimes happens that one expert reliably comes up with structuple assignments that work empirically, whereas the codings of other experts are not reflected in the data. Elizur's coding of advancement as cognitive did work empirically, whereas classifying this work value as affective or instrumental would not (as well). In this case, one faces the task of explicating in which particular way that one expert understands the facets or whether he or she possibly uses additional facets as supplementary criteria for coding.

Structuple assignments become easier as facets become clearer. Ambiguities are typically a consequence of vague facets or facets that are too complex or undifferentiated. Items, similarly, may also be too complex, as previously discussed. One cannot say, however, what is an appropriate level of differentiation for facets and items without specifying the purpose. In social psychology, for example, it is often sufficient to distinguish between cognitive, affective, and instrumental behavior. Indeed, a number of empirical laws (e.g., in attitude research) relate to this typology of behaviors. In other contexts, however, one may need much finer behavior classes that essentially break up these behavior types into subtypes.

Changing the facet system also changes these structuples, of course. Yet structuples may also have to be reconsidered if the data "refuse" to behave accordingly. If, for example, an item in an intelligence test that was classified as arithmetical consistently behaves as verbal items and not as the other arithmetical items (as may well happen, e.g., in an arithmetical problem that is presented verbally), one would be well advised to study the rule by which one discriminates between arithmetical and verbal items.

Constructing Concrete Items

Facet systems define classes of items or item types. For each item type there are generally infinite by many concrete items. This is so because the item types are characterized only by a small set of conceptual characteristics that leave many degrees of freedom for constructing concrete items. How, then, should one proceed in such constructions?

Verbal items serve as a good example because they are most problematic. The factorial survey approach restricts itself to presenting a compactly phrased version of the structuples as stimuli. Market researchers, similarly, often use commodity bundles in conjoint measurement approaches, that is, objects such as store $x = $ (10% rebate, limited parking space, 5 minutes away from home, average selection), and ask the respondents to evaluate them (Jackson, 1983). These methods quickly become impractical if the number of facets goes up and if the structs become more abstract.

In contrast, consider the following. Subjects usually have no problem judging how embarrassing it would be if they were to meet their boss in an adult book store. According to Borg, Staufenbiel, and Scherer (1987) the subject, in this situation, violates numerous norms and assumes that these violations are attributed to him or her by an important reference group as a personal weakness. Obviously, one could not ask a respondent directly about his or her embarrassment in a situation characterized in such terms. Rather, it becomes necessary to use concrete examples for this item type.

Concrete items can be formulated rather briefly or in considerable detail and richness. Two examples that we looked at are the relatively lengthy vignette that described situations in forms of a little story and the question, How is your mood these days? The vignette item may have the disadvantage that a person's response is distracted by various irrelevant concrete details. Thus, *error variance* is generated. In the short item type, on the other hand, a response depends critically on the choice of every word the item contains: If they should cause unintended connotations, then there is no further information that may counterbalance this effect and lead the respondent back to what was meant. It is advantageous, in any case, to have more than just one item for each item type in order to arrive at more stable estimates for its responses.

On the Definition of Facet

So far, we have not yet given a formal definition of facet. Guttman (1954c) first defined facet as "a set of elements," but he (1959a) soon modified the definition as "a set that is a component of a Cartesian product." Yet it is easy to see that Guttman (1959a) had more in mind:

> Facet theory generalizes R. A. Fisher's design of experiments to the design of theories, especially of structure. . . . Structural (and other) theories concern themselves with various sets of elements (concepts). Composite concepts are often defined in terms of Cartesian products of simpler sets. By a facet we shall mean a set that is a component of a Cartesian product. No standard term for this appears in the mathematical or other literature. Experience shows the need for such a term, to distinguish the idea involved from related but often radically different concepts denoted by "dimension," "factor," "element," etc. (p. 130)

In that experiments are always set up with a particular hypothesis in mind, it is clear that the notion of facet has always been associated with scientific purposiveness. A purely set-theoretical definition of facet is therefore misleadingly sterile.

The purpose of facets is to promote conceptual and empirical knowledge. If one agrees that "knowledge is knowledge of differences" (Runkel & MacGrath, 1968, p. 51), then facets, first of all, serve to conceptually break up an initially monolithic construct by explicating its different logical and semantic aspects. With clear and reliable facets, this serves the purpose of enhancing conceptual control over a universe of discourse. So, rather than talking about "plants" in general or presenting long lists of specific plants, botanists invented a system of distinctions that makes it easier to keep track of the varieties of plants.

These conceptual distinctions are, moreover, hypothesized to be empirically useful. That is, quite generally, facets are usually hypothesized to make conceptual distinctions that are mirrored in corresponding differences of the data. In experimental design, for example, a facet may play the role of an "independent variable" that always comes with the hypothesis that it accounts for variance in the dependent variable.

Definitional Shifts Between Content Facets and Range Facets

Categorical Mapping

Consider the case in which we have a set of questions, each one with its own particular range, $R1, \ldots, Rn$. The following is an example:

How high is your income these days?

How important is it to you personally to make a lot of money?

We could write these questions as follows, in which the × symbol of the usual Cartesian product notation is replaced by the word *and:*

	R1		R2	
Person (*p*) assesses	(*very high at this time*)		(*very important*)	
his/her income as →	(to)	and	(to)	
	(*very low at this time*)		(*not important*)	

This formulation (*categorical mapping*) closely corresponds to the structure of the usual persons-by-variables data matrix. The domain of this mapping essentially contains only the population, and the range consists of item ranges, in which each range R_i ($i = 1,2$) corresponds to an item.

Structioned Mapping

We can express the above items types in an alternative formulation (*structioned mapping*). This is done by pulling the question part of the items into the domain:

	Q1 = criterion		
	(level of)	object	
Person (*p*) assesses his/her	( )	(income)	
	(notion of importance of)		

Q2 = time			
(in general)	(*very high*)		
( ) →	(. . .)	in the sense of an element of Q1	
(at this time)	(*very low*)		

A structioned mapping has the advantage of clearly bringing out the distinctions that the two items make and those that are built into the items as further potential facets. Explicating such distinctions helps in constructing concrete items. On the other hand, a general range such as {*very high*, . . . , *very low*} would be substantively empty, and thus the range has to refer back to a facet in Q (which is $Q1$ = criterion here). Such a facet is called a *stem* facet of Q. It endows the range with its meaning. The other facets of Q are called *qualifying* (moderating) facets of Q.

A structioned mapping for formally representing items is, therefore, simultaneously simpler and more complicated than a categorical mapping. It usually has advantages if it stimulates a meaningful search for something common in the items. For example, in the given case, it suggests the question whether there is another, general sense in which the range {*very high, . . . , very low*} can be understood. One possibility is that judgments of high income and beliefs in high importance both express a high involvement or high contact with the object income. This would allow one to replace this facet with the new facet {*high, . . . , low*} *contact with object o.*

Range Versus Content Facets

Generally, it would depend on the purpose of the research whether one should turn range facets into content facets. It should always be done in case of a common-meaning range such as the high-low contact range that appears possible here. It becomes more problematic when the researcher throws all kinds of "background variables" into the domain by facetizing P accordingly. A mapping sentence such as this is sometimes set up in order to bring all variables of the design together. Consider the following:

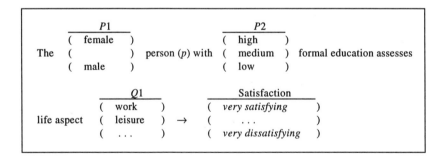

As concrete items, one could take, for example, "I like my job very much," "I am looking forward to going to work every morning," or "I never get bored in my leisure time," each one with the range {*agree very much, . . . , disagree very much*}. Obviously, the facets gender and education do not appear in these items. Indeed, they actually represent range facets of other items that ask for demographic characteristics:

Demographics			R1		R2	
(	1. gender	)	(female	)	(higher	)
(p) has (		) →	(male	)	(medium	)
(	2. education	)			(low	)

It is advantageous to completely take out these background variables from the above mapping sentence and construct two mapping sentences—one that specifies the facets of Q (content facets) and simply (p) and another one that explicates the P-facets as range facets as shown. The reason being that both mapping sentences are directly related to the actual items of the study. Possible hypotheses on the effect of background variables are also easy to specify in terms of the ranges Satisfaction, R1, and R2.

The mapping sentence in the previous box can be further simplified, of course. One can replace R1 and R2 by gender and education, and thus reduce the domain of the mapping sentence to simply (p). This results in a bare-bones categorical mapping sentence, in which the items correspond to the facets of the range:

	Gender		Education	
	(female	)	(higher	)
(p) →	(male	)	(medium	)
			(low	)

This reduction is, in a sense, the reversal of what one often tries to do in setting up a structioned mapping sentence for the "foreground" variables: one starts with a simple categorical mapping sentence and then attempts to pull the content of the items into the domain of a structioned mapping sentence.

Facet Separation Principle

As a simple guide to formulating efficient and lucid mapping sentences, Shye & Elizur (1994) proposed the following *facet separation principle:*

Domain content facets classify questions (stimuli), range facets classify persons (respondents).

One can always adhere to this guiding principle if one has a scientific hypothesis in mind; for then, strictly speaking, no background variables are of interest. Consider the following example from Shye and Elizur (1994). The researcher wants to study spatial intelligence of male and female persons. Written as a categorical mapping sentence, the researcher wants to assess:

		Spatial Intelligence	Gender	
		(very high)	(female)	
(*p*)	→	(...)	(male)	
		(very low)		

The variable gender, which is often considered a background or demographic variable, is included here as an ordered foreground variable because (for the sake of the example) it is hypothesized that men are better in spatial intelligence than women. This hypothesis is biologically explained as the consequence of men's senso-motoric endowment that is more oriented toward behavior in space ("hunter"). Spatial intelligence as well as "maleness" (of sensomotoric endowment) may thus be taken as elements of a facet modality of space orientation. In a mapping sentence with common range this is expressed as follows:

	Modality			
	(spatial intelligence)	(strongly)		
(*p*) is through his/her (	) → (...)	space-oriented		
	(sensomotoric maleness)	(weakly)		

The original question on a dimension of intelligence, spatial intelligence, in combination with the variable gender has now been turned into a more abstract question that aims at a particular space disposition with two modalities. In fact, this illustrates that even a variable such as gender is not automatically a background variable. Rather, it is part of a definitional system of observations for testing a hypothesis.

A Second Look at *P*-Facetization

As the facet separation principle suggests, there is no technical distinction between background (e.g., demographic variables) items and research items (drawn from the studied content universe). Every background variable, as well as every researched item, through its respective (response) range, classifies the elements of P. Hence, facetizations of P are effected by the range facets, whereas the content universe is facetized by content facets $Q1, \ldots, Qn$. But, though the assignment of structuples to Q's elements concerns the definitional (design) part of the study and is conducted by conceptual analysis, the assignment of structuples to P's elements concerns the empirical part of the study, and is conducted by observation.

5 Mapping Sentences

- General Notions
- Cumulative Research and Mapping Sentences
- Number of Facets in Mapping Sentences
- Goodness Criteria for Mapping Sentences
- On Constructing Good Mapping Sentences
- Exactness of a Mapping Sentence

General Notions

Many applications of FT, particularly those that involve experimental designs, only specify a number of facets of Q and P as independent variables to study their effects on R. Borg et al. (1986), for example, surmised that the embarrassment that a subject feels in a particular event depends on the following three facets:

Actor	Content	Actor's Responsibility
(subject him/herself)	(body: looks)	(not responsible)
(p from primary group)	(body: functional)	(responsible, not intentional)
($\bar{p}$ from secondary group)	(sex)	(responsible and intentional)
	(skills: motor)	
	(skills: intellectual)	
	(skills: social)	
	(morals)	
	(clothes)	

They constructed descriptions for situations that varied on these facets. For example, for the structuple 263 = (p from primary group, social skills, responsible and intentional), the following item was set up: "I brought a

49

friend home. As we sit with my family at the dinner table, he cracks a dirty joke." The respondents were asked how embarrassing such a situation would be for them.

The data showed that the three facets did not allow one to explain the observations very well. An important reason for this failure lies in the insufficient clarity of the design: All we have are three facets but they are simply listed without specifying how they are related to each other and what roles they are supposed to play vis-à-vis the range. This leads to difficulties in constructing concrete items for the structuples because a structuple such as 263 simply does not specify precisely enough what properties a concrete item is required to possess. To achieve this, structioned mapping sentences are used.

A mapping sentence, as we have discussed previously, is a combination of formal and informal language. Its formal elements are the facets. Its informal parts—for example, the verbal connectives—often contain aspects of the design that at the moment are not so much at the focus of the research interest. Rather, they serve to give the facets a context in which their roles become clearer. Furthermore, the informal parts of the mapping sentence usually play an important role in cumulative research, because to explicate them often offers a natural starting point for further control strategies.

The power of mapping sentences is immediately apparent when the previously discussed embarrassment facets are compared with the corresponding mapping sentence developed by Borg et al. (1987):

```
(p) believes that,     ( comprehensive )              ( focused     )
   in a situation      (     . . .     )   system of  (    . . .    )   values
   in which a          ( narrow        )              ( not focused )

            ( good, not mean and bad        )
            ( physically skillful, not clumsy )
            ( pretty, not ugly              )
            ( attractive, not repulsive     )
 on being   ( powerful, not a pushover      )   of a reference group (g) that is
            ( civilized, not a hick         )
            ( intelligent, not stupid       )
            ( gutsy, not a wimp             )

 ( important   )           ( strongly )
 (    . . .    )  to (p) is (    . . .  )  ( violated ), and where (p)
 ( unimportant )           ( weakly   )
```

(continued on next page)

```
believes that the (violated) value system is

(  certainly  )  (  important    )                      (  sure     )
(   ...       )  (              )  to (g), and (p) is   (   ...     )
(  possibly   )  (  unimportant  )                      (  not sure )

                 (  strongly  )
that the violation is  (   ...    )  attributed to him/her, feels that
                 (  weakly    )

                       (  very embarrassed   )
he/she would feel   →  (       ...           )
                       (  not embarrassed    )
```

This mapping sentence relates the facets to each other within a meaningful substantive context, actually expressing a cognitive theory of embarrassment. A person's embarrassment is supposed to depend on the values of some reference group that become violated in a particular situation and on how he or she feels that this violation is attributed to him or her by this group. Whether this attribution is just was predicted to be irrelevant, because the facet responsibility showed no effect in the previous study (Borg et al., 1986).

The reason for placing *violated* in parentheses is that we want to suggest that this element could be generalized into a facet such as {violated, satisfied}. This establishes situations for which a generalization of the range from {*very embarrassed, . . . , not embarrassed*} to {*very embarrassed, . . . , very proud*} seems appropriate. In any case, we see that a mapping sentence is weighted with more meaning than simple listings of unrelated facets and thereby helps to further hypotheses with much less effort and in a more coordinated fashion.

Using this structioned mapping sentence as a basis, concrete items were constructed that varied on the facets' *comprehensiveness* (of value system), *strength of violation,* and *strength of attribution.* It turned out that it was easier to construct the items than before simply because the concepts were clearer. Explicating the facets that were not used in the items also helped because it was clear what should be held constant. Not surprisingly, the correspondence of the data to this design also came out much clearer.

As another example for showing the power of mapping sentences for integrating facets into a conceptual context, consider again the Bastide and van den Berghe (1957) items discussed in Chapter 4. Extending the modality facet to the usual three elements, a mapping sentence for these items could be formulated as follows:

$$A = modality$$

	(emotional)	
The (White) person (p) assesses in	(cognitive)	terms the behavior of
	(action tendency)	

$B = reference\ group$			$C = relation$
(Whites in general)	relating to Blacks by	(making comparisons)
(person p him/herself)		(hypothetically interacting)

$$R = range$$

	(very positive)	
$\rightarrow$	(...)	toward the behavior
	(very negative)	

This mapping sentence helps to clarify the object of the attitude (relational behavior). It shows more clearly than a listing of facets that Facet A is a modifier of p's attitudinal response itself, whereas Facets B and C are modifiers of the attitude object. It also suggests various ways to extend and generalize this mapping sentence by further facets.

Cumulative Research and Mapping Sentences

The semantics of the embarrassment mapping sentence are relatively complex, and it is quite obvious that a simple listing of its facets is insufficient for constructing or culling concrete items. On the other hand, if one has only a few facets, it may appear to be pretentious formalism to embed them into a mapping sentence. Yet as seen from a cumulative research perspective, an explicated mapping sentence often makes subsequent work easier. Consider the following example. Levy (1976) reports a mapping sentence for different questions on subjective well-being that reads (slightly modified) similar to the following:

	($e1$ = primary)	
(p) assesses his/her satisfaction with his/her	( )	environment
	($e2$ = secondary)	

	($a1$ = work)		
	($a2$ = family)	(very high)	
in life area	($a3$ = friends) $\rightarrow$	(...)	satisfaction
	($a4$ = education)	(very low)	
	($a5$ = health)		
	($a6$ = in general)		

The roles of the two facets, *environment* and *life areas,* are simple here. Both of them modify, independently of each other, the object for which a judgment is to be made, that is, his or her subjective well-being or satisfaction.

Note that the mapping sentence has a feature that may lead to confusion: The element $a6$ actually is a set rather than a simple object. That is, $a6$ contains all of the elements $a1$ to $a5$ as its elements. Formally, this poses no problem, because all that is required of a set's elements is that they be distinct. They need not be disjoint (non-overlapping).

Employing an element such as $a6$ = in general is useful if one plans to formulate items in such a way that they comprehensively refer to all the different life areas. If, on the other hand, items are constructed that make no special reference to these life areas, then it would be better to use $a6$ = unspecified instead. This formulation makes clearer that a $a6$ item should be constructed by skipping all particular references to the facet life area. If one wants, on the other hand, to construct items that explicitly ask for judgments on certain collections of A's elements, then such collections have to be specified as elements of a revised Facet A. In Levy's study, it would be easy to show that both the environment and the life area facets lead to clear-cut organizations of the data. It, therefore, makes sense to think about the next step in which the mapping sentence technique has been found particularly useful. Mapping sentences are usually richer in meaning than a listing of unconnected facets. They often suggest quite naturally various ways to proceed, such as making the given facets more precise, differentiating them further by adding new facets to the design (*intension*), or by extending the facets to include additional elements (*extension*).

Levy and Guttman (1975) made use of each of these to arrive at the following mapping sentence:

	($a1$: cognitive)		($b1$: state of)
(p)'s	( )	assessment of	( )
	($a2$: affective)		($b2$: government's treatment of)

the well-being of his/her social (reference) group

($c1$. self)		($d1$. primary internal)	
($c2$. government)		($d2$. primary social)	environment,
($c3$. state)	with respect	($d3$. primary resource)	concerning a
($c4$. institution)	to the	($d4$. neighborhood)	
($c5$. new immigrants)		($d5$. town)	
($c6$. poor)		($d6$. state)	
($c7$. other individuals)		($d7$. world)	
($c8$. unspecified)			

(continued on next page)

		($f1$. recreation)
		($f2$. family)
		($f3$. on the whole)
		($f4$. security)
($e1$. general)		($f5$. health)
( ) aspect of life area		($f6$. economy)
($e2$. specific)		($f7$. education)
		($f8$. religion)
		($f9$. society)
		($f10$. immigration)
		($f11$. work)
		($f12$. information)
		($f13$. communication)

according to p's normative criterion for this life area

$\rightarrow$ ($\quad$ *very satisfactory* $\quad$)
($\qquad$ ... $\qquad$) in the sense of the element from facet B
($\quad$ *very unsatisfactory* $\quad$)

Comparing this second-generation mapping sentence with its predecessor, it becomes clear that the old environment facet has been differentiated into an ordered facet with seven elements: $d1$-$d3$ correspond to the old category primary environment, $d4$-$d7$ to the old secondary environment. As to Facet D, Levy and Guttman (1975) write:

> In this research, environmental facet D is treated as an ordered facet. The elements are ranked in terms of "distance" from the respondent himself. For example, the "state" is defined to be a secondary framework for "self" (of the respondent), and is more distant from "self" than is a primary environment such as mood. (p. 366)

The life area facet is contained in both mapping sentences. The new mapping sentence simply extends it by adding a few additional elements. Other modifications in the mapping sentence can be traced by the reader.

Number of Facets in Mapping Sentences

Mapping sentences such as the previous one are typical for advanced research. They often contain many facets and allow thousands of different ways to read them, implying thousands of possible structuples or types of questions. Indeed, the number of possible concrete questions is almost always infinite, because for each question type, one can generally come up with incredibly many concrete items.

But, then, how many facets are needed? Kernberg et al. (1972), for example, studied the complex question, "how the process of psychotherapy brought about changes in the suffering patient" (p. v). They note in their final research report that

> one of the interesting results of the entire facet analysis was the fact that complex variables such as those needed to measure behaviors, treatments, etc., could be described by only 16 basic sets of elements and that every variable could then be defined in terms of this basic framework. (p. 92)

This "result" is the consequence that the Cartesian product of these 16 facets—most of them quite simple ones with only four or fewer elements—contains over 278 billion elements. With good facets, it should not be too difficult to classify even the most complex phenomena with such a detailed definitional system.

Goodness Criteria for Mapping Sentences

What, then, are "good" facets? First, good facets should be clear, so that different experts on the respective content would be able to reliably classify items with them into the same categories. (Such agreement could be measured empirically.) Second, good facets should not only be useful conceptually in structuring a universe of discourse, but also serve to structure the data that they characterize. This means that the facets should be "mirrored" in some aspects of the data. In that mapping sentences serve to clarify the facets of the research question and their roles with respect to the range, their goodness depends critically on the goodness of their facets.

Yet good mapping sentences should possess further properties. They should point beyond the immediate content in not being overly concrete and ad-hoc, but rather somewhat more abstract, so that they can be applied to wider item spaces and larger content domains. For example, we saw in the above embarrassment mapping sentence that it suggested, by a simple extension of its range, that the same facets might be useful in structuring a different domain of interest, that is, pride. Moreover, good mapping sentences should also lend themselves to extensions and generalizations and, thus, help in building cumulative research.

On Constructing Good Mapping Sentences

Formulating a good mapping sentence is usually a demanding task. It requires, above all, excellent insights into the respective subject matter. Even then, a good mapping sentence is often only the end-result of considerable work. Marcus (personal communication, 1983) reports, for example, that his research team spent over half a year to generate a mapping sentence—and items pertinent to it—that was to guide an extensive longitudinal research project on the effects of substance abuse of women on their children (Marcus & Hans, 1982).

The research team started out with an extensive search of the literature. This identified a variety of variables that appeared important for the research questions. The variables were then sorted and integrated into a common conceptual framework that had to be developed along the way. Then, the first mapping sentences were formulated to see which facets should be observed, which ranges should be used, and how the domain facets related to these ranges.

In practice, such tentative first mapping sentences typically develop quickly into monstrous jumbo sentences by adding more and more facets. More depth and more economy are then achieved by reformulating the mapping sentence so that its facets are less descriptive and concrete and more abstract. Such reformulations, moreover, have the advantage that they apply to a variety of situations.

As an example, consider the facet {affective, cognitive, instrumental}, which has been found useful in many different contexts. Shye (1985b; 1989) discusses an even more abstract alternative that is supposed to hold for "action systems" in general. It is evident that such abstractions are hardly obvious at the beginning. Rather, they typically develop in long-range research.

Exactness of a Mapping Sentence

A mapping sentence is always somewhat vague. The lack of precision is an unavoidable consequence of the vagueness of the underlying substantive theory. Theories that describe all of its elements without any ambiguity are not available in the empirical sciences.

In practice, science always proceeds by starting with something vague, and by making its theoretical notions more and more precise in the course of research.

Armchair methodologists sometimes insist that all elements of a theory be made completely unambiguous from the start. Only then would it make sense to construct items. We think that it is more fruitful to think of a highly technical language as a desired end product of research. The scientist involved in practical research ultimately chooses a language whose semantics are sufficiently reliable for what he or she is studying. As Guttman (1991) remarks, the term *affective* is often used in psychology without further definition or differentiation. It is simply taken from everyday language, as are many concepts in psychology. Such a notion, although vague, is sufficiently reliable to carry, for example, attitude research to some extent. Of course, the terms will sooner or later have to replaced with something more precise, particularly if one decides to take a closer look at emotions.

Cumulative theory building, in any case, resembles more a ping-pong process that alternates—or, better, *negotiates*—between conceptual-definitional work on the one hand, and empirical studies on the other. Definitional systems define and structure the universe of content, however vaguely. Observations on this universe are needed to test the correspondence of these definitions to reality. Observations, however, may also serve to modify definitions in what Shepard (1981, p. 26) has called "bidirectional, mutually constraining interaction" and a "cooperative alternation."

Mapping sentences are natural starting points for model building. In fact, most if not all model building begins informally and then becomes more technical and formal. As an example for a mapping sentence phrased in a more technical language, consider the following specimen (Borg, 1994):

	D-strength	*Type of D*	
	(*strong*)	(hunger)	
Rat (*r*) exhibits in maze (*x*) under	( )	( )	and
	(*weak*)	(thirst)	

H-strength
(strong)
(...) habit strength for approach behavior toward the goal box and
(no)

I-strength
(*strong*)   (strong)
(...) incentives → (...) approach behavior toward the goal box
(*weak*)   (no)

Most experimental psychologists should be able to directly communicate about this mapping sentence without much ambiguity because all important terms here are "technical" ones that are understood in the same way by everyone in this profession. Some theorists thought that this mapping sentence could be made even more technical by expressing certain key notions in a "formal" language. Two proposals were made on how the facets of the domain are related to the range facet: $R = (D + I) \times H$ (Spence, 1956) and $R = D \times I \times H$ (Hull, 1952), in which R = response strength, D = drive, I = incentive, and H = habit strength. Hull's version, explicated as a mapping sentence with "operational" terms (e.g., *trial* rather than *habit strength*), reads as follows:

For rat (r) in maze (x) it holds that

$$f_1 \left\{ \begin{matrix} (\ t\ min\ ) \\ (\ \ldots\ ) \\ (\ 0\ min\ ) \end{matrix} \right\} deprivation\ of \left\{ \begin{matrix} (\ water\ ) \\ \\ (\ food\ ) \end{matrix} \right\} \times f_2 \left\{ \begin{matrix} (\ m\ reward\ units\ ) \\ (\ \ldots\ ) \\ (\ 0\ reward\ units\ ) \end{matrix} \right\}$$

$$\times f_3 \left\{ \begin{matrix} (\ n\ trials\ ) \\ (\ \ldots\ ) \\ (\ 0\ trials\ ) \end{matrix} \right\} in\ (x) = f_4\ \{k\ units\ of\ performance\}\ \text{of approach behavior toward goal box, in which } f_1, \ldots, f_4 \text{ are strictly increasing real-valued functions, given } t < \text{max.}$$

The side constraint $t < $ max prevents excessive deprivation, which should not be so long that performance goes down as a consequence of physical weakness or death. One could account for this by allowing for a turning point on f_1 or by even specifying a particular parametric function type with such a property. Picking such a function, however, requires (lots of) data and thus asks for empirical research.

The example shows that formalizing a mapping sentence automatically leads to a mathematical model. Such models are approached in FT in a bottom-up way, starting with substantive considerations on definitions and distinctions, not by formalizing idealized cases. The proper level of formalization depends on the level of knowledge in the respective content domain, but also on the audience's mastery of technical and formal terms.

How far one should go in formalizing a mapping sentence depends on the level of knowledge in the respective substantive domain, its precision of key terms, and on the people to whom one wants to communicate the results of the research. Borrowing an analogy by Guttman (1991) in this context, we can illustrate this as follows.

An architect would possibly present most effectively his or her design of a house to a client by drawing some pictures of the planned house, together with trees and people. Once the client gets the idea, more technical diagrams on the layout of the rooms or the electrical wiring may be appropriate, but it may need competent commentaries by the architect to be understood correctly.

Analytical diagrams, finally, that explicate, for example, civil engineering computations on the statics of the house, are even more formal. They have, on the other hand, much more precise implications, but only for the expert. Mapping sentences are similar in this sense: Those that are written in normal everyday language are easy to communicate to everyone, but leave much room for interpretation; a more technical language increases precision and is more compact, but requires more expertise on the part of the reader. An analytical language, finally, requires substantial technical training not only on content but also on form (e.g., mathematics), but it also carries very far.

Common Range

- The Notion of a Common Range
- The Common Range in the Development of Mapping Sentences

The Notion of a Common Range

Consider the question, What is true for country *x?* together with five different ranges: (a) {*very small, . . . , very large*} *GNP*, (b) {*low, . . . , high*} *child mortality rate*, (c) {*few, . . . , many*} *students*, (d) {*no, . . . , many*} *illiterates*, and (e) {*no, . . . , many*} *mainframe computers*. It is easy to see that each range not only assesses a particular aspect of country *x*, but also that they are all related as indicators of the level of development of that country. Hence, each range element could be mapped once more onto this *common range* (CR)—that is, onto {*high, . . . , low*} *level of development*.

Generally, we have a CR for a set of items if (a) the range for every item is ordered, and (b) all ranges are monotonically related to a common substantive criterion. To see whether different ranges have a common range, it is useful to first formulate, as facets of *Q*, those aspects in which they differ. That is always possible. We obtain for our example:

	Facet A			Facet B	
Respondent (*r*) evaluates the	(GNP (child mortality rate (number of students (percentage of illiterates (number of mainframe computers	)))))	of	(country *a*) (country *b*) (country *c*)	→

(continued on next page)

R1			R2		
(*very large*	)		(*very high*	)	
(...	)	in the sense of facet *A* →	(...	)	level of
(*very small*	)		(*very low*	)	development

In practice, the respondent only delivers mappings from Q to $R1$. The mapping from $R1$ to $R2$ is specified by the researcher. As has been noted elsewhere (Shye & Elizur, 1976, 1994), the same item, or set of items, may be interpreted to assess different $R2$s (i.e., $R2$s with different meanings), depending on the investigated concept. Thus, for example, the question "What is the GNP of country x?" could be interpreted as assessing, along with other appropriate items, country x's economic strength. It could also be interpreted as simply a notion of size or the geographical knowledge of the respondent.

Now consider the question "How large is country x?" If we include this question into the mapping sentence above, then the $R1$ range loses its common meaning even though it is formally unchanged. This shows that an equivalent or even identical wording for a range is not sufficient for establishing a CR. Nor, for that matter, is it necessary, because the actual ranges for, say, the GNP and the-number-of-students questions could be estimates in dollars and ratings such as 1 = many and 0 = few, respectively. Both relate monotonically to the CR. A CR is established by substantive considerations on the *common meaning* of the ranges.

In practice, it would be unusual, however, to discover a CR in a set of items. Typically, one proceeds the other way around; that is, one starts out with a CR derived from what one wants to study. If one is interested, for example, in attitude behavior toward a certain object, then one first defines as a CR for all items the scale {*very negative, . . . , very positive*} *behavior toward this object* (see Chapter 7 for more on attitude items). Differences among the items then relate to differences in finer aspects of the questions asked.

The same is true for intelligence items. They must all assess intelligence—that is, be monotonically related, by definition, to the range {*very wrong, . . . , very right*} *according to an objective rule* (see Chapter 7 for more on intelligence items). The exact wording of the particular range for each item can vary widely.

In both examples, the CR serves to distinguish the universe of interest from other universes. That does not mean that in empirical studies one must only have items with a single common range. Often, the opposite is true: Many studies investigate the structure of different universes and relationships between them.

It is a common fallacy to assume that empirical "multidimensionality" somehow disproves the hypothesis of a common range. Intelligence items are, for example, multidimensional, but this relates to their differences in Q only. The common-rangeness of these items is related to the hypothesis that all intelligence test items correlate positively among each other. In fact, it constitutes a rationale for such a hypothesis (see Chapter 10). The CR, therefore, is in a sense related to the *similarity* of the items, whereas the facets of Q correspond to *differences* among the items. In the conceptual system, this is so by definition; for the data, this is a hypothesis.

The Common Range in the Development of Mapping Sentences

One normally begins to develop a mapping sentence with a preliminary definition of a common range. Marcus, Hans, Patterson, and Morris (1983), for example, set out to study the damage to a child caused by fetal exposure to opioid drugs. This led them to first define in what sense they wanted to look at the children. They then define a range in terms of the "level of functioning" of a child:

$$
R1 \quad = \quad
\begin{pmatrix} good \\ \dots \\ poor \end{pmatrix}
\quad \text{level of functioning of the child}
$$

$R1$ immediately leads to the next question: What distinctions can be made with respect to the level of functioning? and, furthermore, when is this observation made? The research team decided to consider the facets contained in the following mapping sentence (somewhat simplified here):

The level of
$\begin{pmatrix} c1 = \text{cognitive} \\ c2 = \text{affective} \\ c3 = \text{instrumental} \begin{pmatrix} c31 = \text{biological} \\ c32 = \text{social} \\ c33 = \text{motor} \end{pmatrix} \end{pmatrix}$ functioning

(continued on next page)

```
            (   prenatal    )
            (   1 day       )
            (   1 month     )              (   feeding   )
  at age    (   4 months    )  in situation (   diapering )   → R1
            (   8 months    )              (   . . .     )
            (   12 months   )
            (   18 months   )
```

The study contained assessments of the child's attentional preferences (c1), of its responses to separation from mother (c2), of walking skills (c33), of clearness of communication with mother (c32), of heart rate responsivity (c31), and of consolability (c32).

For assessing the conditions for the child's level of functioning, a different range is needed:

```
         (   favorable   )
  R2 = (      . . .      )  conditions for a good level of functioning
         (   unfavorable )
```

*R*2 leads to at least two facets that distinguish (a) the "kind of condition" (resource) for a good level of functioning, and (b) the "owner" of this resource. This is written as follows:

	Owner	Kind of Resource	
	($a1$ = parental	($b1$ = ecological)	
The level of	($a2$ = infant	($b2$ = biological)	resource
	($a3$ = family	($b3$ = psychological health)	
		($b4$ = behavioral)	

at time (*t*)   →   R2

(Marcus et al., 1983, differentiate further—e.g., b1 is split into b11 = SES, b12 = housing, and b13 = social support network. We will skip these here.)

In looking at the two mapping sentences that have been established—one with the *R*1 range and another one with *R*2—one might ask if they can be combined into one or if there is a common range for both of them? If "good functioning" itself is conceived as a resource for future good functioning, then one can set up a combined mapping sentence. Consider, first, a version that closely follows a proposal made by Marcus and Hans (1982) and then propose a new formulation. Making use of the above abbreviations, the mapping sentence by Marcus and Hans (1982) reads as follows:

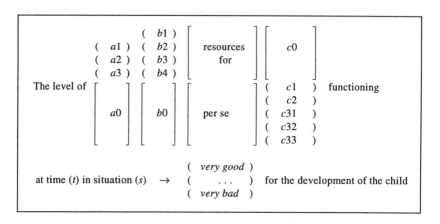

Before we turn to the meaning of the new elements (a0, b0, etc.), we note that this mapping sentence is more complicated than those that we have encountered up to now because the facets are not completely crossed with each other. We have indicated by the brackets that, for example, a0 only goes with its horizontal neighbors b0, per se, and the elements c1, ..., c33 of Facet C. Where we have parentheses rather than brackets, all combinations are possible. Such a case in which certain combinations must be excluded for logical or substantive reasons occurs occasionally in practice (see, e.g., Jordan, 1971), yet, such complicated designs are most often a consequence of the facets one has chosen at the start. By reformulating them, the design can typically be changed into a factorial one.

To see how such reformulations can be accomplished here, first consider the meaning and the role of the yet undefined elements. To be able to combine the two mapping sentences into one, Marcus and Hans (1982) introduced a few place holders (a0, b0, c0) that they called *per se* in each case. The purpose of these elements is easiest to see if one reads to upper part of the mapping sentence: "The level of the a*i*-owned, b*j*-kind resources for the c0-aspect of functioning ... ," which indicates that c0 should be understood as "unspecified."

It is more difficult to understand the bottom half: "The level of the per se-owned, per se-kind, per se . . ." Apparently, the authors wanted to neutralize or skip the respective facets. Again, setting a0 and b0 equal to unspecified serves this purpose better. Moreover, using an element such as per se actually turns the facet into an informal one, because one cannot decide on the basis of the facet's name whether such an element belongs to the facet. For example, for facet *A* = owner of resource, it is clear that *parents, child, family* all belong to *A,* in that they are all owners, whereas per se is not an owner.

Another question concerns the object that is mapped onto the range. In the upper half of the mapping sentence, it is "the resources for a good level of functioning," in the lower half it is "the level of functioning."

The example shows that combining different mapping sentences under one common range is not that simple. In this case, we can, however, design a different version which avoids informal facets, and contains only facets that can be crossed completely. It reads, in long-hand notation, as follows:

The extent to which

                A: agent   B: developmental mode

            (family   )

            (parents   ) (resource-possession (static))

infant (*i*)'s   (self   ) (functioning (dynamic)   ) in the

            (unspecified)

            C: sphere

(unspecified   )

(biological   )

(social   )

(personality   ) sphere at time (*t*) in situation (*s*)

((cognitive   ))

(behavior (affective   ))

((instrumental))

      (*very good*   )

→   (. . .   ) developmental mode (in the sense of an

      (*very bad*   )   element in *B*) of the infant

Formulating an elegant mapping sentence does not require fancy wording, but rather an effort to make the semantics as simple as possible. If one succeeds in this respect, then the range would clearly refer back to a facet of the domain (the stem facet), as Shye (1978b) has stipulated. The proposed mapping sentence covers what Marcus and Hans (1982) probably intended in their report. But our mapping sentence also covers adjacent content universes that the researchers may want to consider, namely the functionings of the infant's immediate social environment (parents, family). Can these functionings, in addition to resources, affect the functioning of the infant?

It is worth noting what we have done here to simplify the design: We placed conditions for functioning, and functioning itself, as elements of a single facet, suggesting that they are both modes, or aspects, of a single notion—development. Indeed, resources may well be considered a manifestation of a generalized notion of development that includes what has taken place in the infant's background. This generalized notion of development endows the new common range with its meaning (compare with maleness and spatial intelligence in Chapter 4).

7 Items

General Notions

The term *item* has no fixed meaning in the social sciences. It usually refers to a specific task in a psychological test or to a verbal question in a questionnaire.[1] In FT, an item is defined as an *observational question together with its range of admissible answers.* The notion of question is meant generically. A question is not only a verbal one presented to a person, but any kind of "query to Nature." Hence, the tasks in an intelligence test are questions, and even an experimental situation that one constructs to observe certain behavior, is a question.

In the context of the Hull-Spence learning experiments (see Chapter 5), each item is an instance of a particular experimental condition (d,h,i) from the universe $D \times H \times I$, together with its range $R = \{strong, \ldots, weak\}$ *appetitive behavior.* Yet there is a subtle difference in connotation between a question with a response range (a variable) and an item. The former is usually referred to in and for itself. The latter, item, is presumed to belong to a set of items pertaining to some content universe, that is, having a common range.

67

Defining Constructs by Defining Items

There are different ways to define a domain of interest. If its elements are observable, the simplest way to define them is to "point at them" by way of a complete listing of its elements. If, however, the domain builds on a construct, then one has to specify its properties more abstractly.

Possibly the method used most frequently in this case is to relate the construct to other notions that are supposedly already known or better known, similar to what a dictionary does. Consider the construct *attitude*. Nominal definitions for attitude often begin as in the following: An attitude is a relatively stable disposition to respond . . . Operational definitions, in contrast, do not specify what the construct is but "relate a concept to what would be observed if certain operations are performed under specified conditions on specified objects" (Aschoff, Gupta, & Minas, 1962, p. 141).

A third way, the *mapping definition,* is chosen in FT (Guttman, 1991; Shye & Elizur, 1994). Here, the construct is defined by specifying the set of all items that assess it. So, for example, one does not concentrate directly on the construct intelligence itself, but rather delineates the universe of intelligence items as the set of all items on an individual's behavior whose range is {*very right, . . . , very wrong*} *according to an objective rule*. Such an approach is similar to operational definitions insofar as it puts conceptual considerations directly into a language that is closely related to actual empirical research. On the other hand, it avoids equating the construct with a particular measurement operation, which raises the problem of how to relate the many, say, "intelligences" that are emerging with every new measurement operation (Suppe, 1973).

At first sight, defining items rather than constructs seems to avoid partly the definitional issue by talking around the topic. Yet looking more carefully, one notes that this is true for all definitions. No definition directly says what the construct is; rather, it uses some form of triangulation in semantic space. In formal concept analysis, for example, a concept is defined by a set of properties that leads to lattices of super- and subconcepts (Wille, 1982).

Some Special Item Universes

Intelligence Items

In the social sciences, items usually ask for a person's behavior of some kind in a particular class of situations. The items in a psychological test partially define such a situation. Take the question, How much is $1 + 1$? It looks like an intelligence item, but exactly how is this decided?

A person p may react to the question, $1 + 1 = ?$ in several ways. Each of these reactions could be recorded as a datum. One could, for example, record p's galvanic skin response, p's reaction time until he or she gives an answer, p's nonverbal reactions to the questions, or all of p's verbal productions following the question. One such production could be the answer "Two"; another, the remark "Leave me alone!" If we restrict ourselves to verbal responses and to those of numbers, then this aspect of p's behavior is intelligence behavior according to the following mapping definition (simplified from Guttman, in Gratch, 1973):

> An item belongs to the universe of intelligence items if and only if it asks about behavior that is assessed on the range {*very right . . . very wrong*} according to an objective rule.

If a person gives the answer "Two," then this answer is "right" in terms of common arithmetics. If the answer is "Zero," then it is "wrong" by the same criterion. It is right, however, in terms of modulo-2 arithmetics. In any case, the behavior is intelligence behavior, because each arithmetics is composed of rules that allow one to objectively assess such a numerical answer on the range that characterizes intelligence items. Assessments with the categories *more* or *less right* (*wrong*) are easy to define—for example, by using a measure of deviation of the given answer from the correct one.

It is interesting to look at the original version of this definition owed to Guttman (1965b):

> An act of a subject is intelligent to the (extent) to which it is classified by a (tester) as (demonstrating) a correct perception of an unexhibited logical (aspect) of a (relation) intended by the tester, on the basis of another (exhibited) logical (aspect) of that relation that is correctly perceived by the subject. (p. 26)

The parentheses are in the original text; they denote facets of the item questions that could be further expanded.

For two of the facets, Guttman explicates the following distinctions: (a) Demonstrate and exhibit are related to the facet *language of communication* = {verbal, symbolic, pictorial}; (b) Aspect is differentiated into *content of communication* = {analytical or rule-finding, performance or rule-application}. Furthermore, Guttman comments that

> there are many possible facets. For example, within arithmetic—or even within addition alone—the number of digits per number is a facet. The number of numbers to be added is also a facet. Thus addition by itself is an infinite domain (p. 28).

This makes clear that mapping definitions typically have their own history. Guttman's original version was only a beginning. It is overloaded with irrelevant content facets and, therefore, more a mapping sentence than a definition. The newer definition above is minimalistic: its domain (behavior) is generally valid for psychological research, and its distinguishing substance rests with the specification of the range. In fact, the mapping definition focuses on delineating a common range for all items of interest.

Formulating an abstract definition for items such as the one for intelligence items opens the way for further conceptual work. Jensen (personal communication, 1994) suggested that our definition for intelligence items may be too general. His counter-example was that "holding the door open for someone" could be considered right in terms of an objective rule, namely "etiquette." This example leads to several lines of thought. First, one could question whether this type of behavior should be considered intelligence behavior. (Is it intelligence behavior in the sense of "social intelligence"?) Second, one may try to enhance the reliability of the definition and attempt to explicate criteria for what constitutes an objective rule. Third, the above range for intelligence items could be restricted, for example, by invoking a modifying facet for the rule. Guttman (1965a) proposed that rules could be classified by the facet {logical, factual, semantic}, so any rule that does not fall into one of these three categories is automatically excluded. One could also pull almost any domain facet that does not contain an "unspecified" or an "in general" category into the items' domain, because it almost certainly does not cover all possible classes and, therefore, implicitly acts as a filter or restrictor. (Domain facets, therefore, often implicitly restrict the item universe.)

Attitude Items

Now admit the comment "Leave me alone!" as a legitimate answer to our question, $1 + 1 = ?$ It might be argued that with such an answer the question becomes an attitude item. Attitudes items differ from intelligence items only by their range:

> An item belongs to the universe of attitude items if and only if it asks about behavior which is assessed on the range {*very positive, . . . , very negative*} toward an object.

What, then, is the "object" of our question $1 + 1 = ?$ Formally, it is the question itself, as well as its unexplicated context. Looking more closely and substantively one notes, however, that it is necessary to take into account which range is being used. If an answer such as "Leave me alone!" is an admissible one, the object to which an attitude is expressed could be the interviewer. Yet the object could also be mathematics, or simplistic questions. Each of these objects, once agreed upon, should be common to all items of a single content universe.

Attitude, in any case, is defined by characterizing its items, and these items all map behavior into a particular range. Guttman originally added the domain facet {affective, cognitive, action} behavior, thereby emphasizing that he wanted to abolish the usual restriction of the term *behavior* to *action behavior*. This seemingly idiosyncratic extension throws some light on the role of definitions in FT (Guttman, 1982e):

> The reason for the adoption was not merely because the new definition was clear, but also because it had already been demonstrated to work well in a partnership that succeeded in actually establishing a scientific law for human behavior (p. 332). . . . My definition of attitude was based on the First Law of Attitude and further faceted laws. (p. 342; see Chapter 9 for this law).

So, there is reason not to easily give up this definition and its domain extension to all behavior modalities. One can even argue that "only if a law of behavior which depends on a particular definition is established is there a scientific reason for consensus in adopting that definition" (Guttman, 1991, p. 17). Thus, with Guttman's domain extension for attitude items, the often-asked question how attitude and behavior are related means that one is asking about the relations among affective, cognitive, and action (instrumental) forms of attitudinal behavior.

Many definitions of attitude contain passages such as "a relatively stable disposition to respond . . ." In doing so, they automatically exclude every behavior as nonattitudinal for which one has not shown that it is (relatively) stable over time. Moreover, if one does not specify a particular way of responding, then all relatively stable dispositions to respond are attitudes, including income or locus-of-control convictions. These points show the advantage of our definition. It is wide enough not to restrict empirical research. Indeed, many features of common textbook definitions—such as stability—can now be seen as empirically testable hypotheses. But our definition is also narrow enough to keep the notion of attitude in agreement with intuition.

Principal Components of Attitudes

In the social science literature, one occasionally finds the notion of principal components of attitudes. This idea goes back to Guttman (1954c) who referred by this name to a formal consequence of having a "scalable attitude": If attitude items are scalable in the sense that they allow for a one-dimensional scalogram, then the i-th principal component has a functional relationship to the attitude ("Guttman") scale with $i - 1$ turning points. The first principal component has a monotone functional relationship to the attitude scale, the second one a U-shaped curve (see Figure 7.1 for an example), the third one has two turning points (N-shape), the fourth looks like an M or a W (Figure 7.2), and so forth.

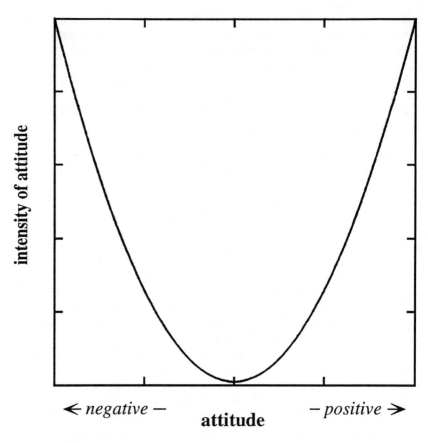

Figure 7.1. Strength of Attitude as a Second Principal Component of Attitude

Only scalability of attitude items can be tested empirically. If it holds, it implies the principal components on purely mathematical grounds. One can, however, ask the nontrivial question whether there exist particular classes of behavior that always have U-, N-, or M-shaped regression curves with respect to that attitude scale. Because of their analogy to the mathematical functional relationships described above, these behaviors are then called second, third, and so forth, principal components of the attitude. This may not be very fortunate terminology, but it serves to point out that all of these components are but different aspects of a person's behavior toward a given object.

A U-shaped relation is found if one compares assessments of behavior toward an object on the positive-negative range with assessments of this same behavior in terms of strong-weak. It is well established that persons

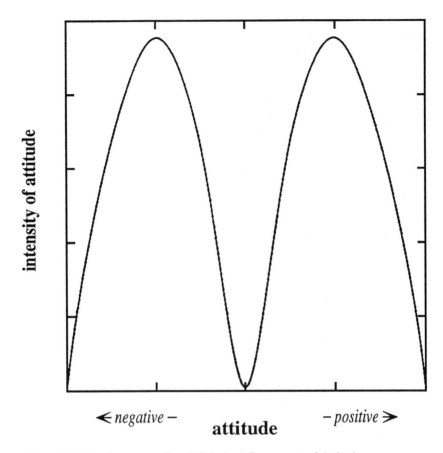

Figure 7.2. Involvement as Fourth Principal Component of Attitude

with very negative or very positive attitudes toward some object also generally have relatively strong attitudes. In other words, those who are relatively neutral about something, are not likely to express strong behavior toward the object in question. Consequently, strength of behavior toward the object is a second principal component of attitude.

Another principal component of attitude, the fourth, is the involvement of a person with an object, defined as behavior with the range {*very much, . . . , very little*} *contact with this object.* Guttman (1954c) argues that,

> if a person is not involved, he should ordinarily be neutral; but, if he should venture an opinion one way or the other, even though he is not involved, this will be unreasoned or "prejudiced," and hence be most extreme—either positively or negatively. (p. 244f)

Involvement, thus, should have an M-shaped regression curve on the positive-negative continuum. According to Levy (1978), this is true only if the norm on involvement with the attitude object is negative; if this norm is positive, then the trend should be W-shaped.

An alternative reasoning, however, leads to the opposite conclusion: Much contact with an object is likely to be associated with strong convictions and hence with the two ends of the attitude scale. In addition, much contact with an object can also characterize the aloof scholar, the arbiter, or the impartial judge who, nevertheless, remains neutral toward the object.

Judging from results presented in Hofstätter (1966, p. 175), one could also hypothesize that the stability of an attitude is a fourth principal component (W-shaped, in this case).

It is tempting to generalize these notions beyond the domain of attitudes. Consider the following framework, derived from earlier suggestions by Guttman (1983), for mapping sentences:

$$
\begin{array}{lll}
 & \underline{\text{Component}} & \\
 & (\quad c1.\ \text{direction} \quad) & \\
\text{The} & (\quad c2.\ \text{intensity} \quad) & \text{behavior of person } (p) \text{ with respect to} \\
 & (\quad c3.\ \text{differentiation} \quad) & \\
 & (\quad c4.\ \text{involution} \quad) & \\
\end{array}
$$

object (o) is assessed by observer (x) as

$$
\rightarrow \quad
\begin{array}{l}
(\quad \text{high} \quad) \\
(\quad \ldots \quad) \\
(\quad \text{low} \quad)
\end{array}
\ \text{in the sense of} \
\begin{array}{l}
(\quad \text{behavior component } ci \quad) \\
(\quad\quad\quad\quad\quad\quad\quad\quad) \\
(\quad \text{some other, extrinsic range} \quad)
\end{array}
$$

Assessing behavior with respect to one of the components $c1, \ldots, c4$ may be considered measuring behavior on an intrinsic range. Other ranges such as time of response in case of attitudes are extrinsic.

For the intrinsic ranges or components, a more explicit characterization of the behavior components can be proposed based on developments made by Guttman (1954c), Lewin (1938), and other motivational theorists (see, e.g., Atkinson, 1964):

1. direction behavior	toward . . . away from object
2. intensity behavior	strong . . . weak
3. differentiation behavior	open . . . closed to object relative to alternative objects
4. involution behavior	much . . . no contact with object

According to these distinctions, attitudinal behavior, having the positive-negative range (vis-à-vis the same object) is montonically related to direction behavior with its toward-away range. On the other hand, the shape of the regression curve of a behavioral variable does not imply a necessary role as a principal component of attitude toward an object. For example, not every behavior assessed in terms of strong-weak that has a U-shaped relation to an attitude is necessarily a second principal component of that attitude. What one needs to clarify is whether the two behaviors refer to the same object. This is not always easy to decide. Consider an example. Value judgments, in which an individual assesses an object on the range {*very important, . . . , not important*} *to me personally*, have a U-shaped relation to satisfaction measures, given some side constraints (Borg, 1991; Borg & Noll, 1990). The question is whether they have the same object. Satisfaction judgments about "my family," say, are possibly behavior toward the object "my family as compared to what I think it should be." Importance judgments on "my family" are possibly behavior toward "my family as it does relate to my well-being" (instrumental value) or, alternatively, "my family as it should relate to my well-being" (normative value). Only in the latter case could it be argued that the value judgments are the second principal component of the satisfaction judgments.

The Moment Theory of Attitude Components

Shye (1975) proposed the Moment Theory for interpreting all principal components of scalable attitudes. The theory is based on the assumption that when a respondent selects his answer from a given scale of possible answers, his selection is governed by a latent distribution defined on that scale, a distribution which is characteristic to the responding individual. So that if it were possible to present the same question to the same individual many times, then, in general, a frequency distribution over the scale—rather than a single, consistent response—would emerge. Another assumption (in fact, a consequence of the mapping definition of attitude) is that in every attitude response scale there is an intrinsic "zero point" (point of neutral attitude) that splits the scale into a positive part and a negative part.

According to Shye's Moment Theory, the principal components of scalable attitude correspond to properties of the latent distribution as follows:

- The first principal component corresponds to the degree to which the mean of the latent distribution, conditioned on the positive part of the scale exceeds the mean conditioned on the negative part of the scale;

- The second principal component corresponds to the degree to which the mean of the latent distribution on the scale differs from the intrinsic zero, i.e., to the distance of the mean from the intrinsic zero;

- The third principal component corresponds to the degree to which the variance of the latent distribution, conditioned on the positive part of the scale, exceeds the variance conditioned on the negative part of the scale;

- The fourth principal component corresponds to the variance of the latent distribution about the intrinsic zero.

And so on. That is, the principal components of scalable attitude are conceived of as arranged in pairs. The first pair refers to the mean of the latent distribution, the second pair to its variance, and in general the nth pair refers to the nth moment of that distribution. Within each pair, the first component (component of odd order) refers to the "direction of the relevant moment," a notion which is given here a quantitative meaning as the excess of that moment, when conditioned on the positive part of the scale, over that moment when conditioned on the negative part of the scale. The second component within each pair (component of even order) is simply the absolute value of the relevant moment about the intrinsic zero (point of neutral attitude) on the scale.

The following mapping sentence, employing the above terminology, efficiently summarizes the definitional framework for the Moment Theory of the Principal Components of Attitude:

```
         (   direction   )
The      (               )   about the intrinsic zero of the attitude scale of the
         (   magnitude    )

(   first    )
(   second   )
(   third    )   moment of the latent distribution of responses by individual
(     :      )
(     :      )

                                                      (   high   )
(p) on a scale of attitude toward an object (o)    →  (    :     )   in  the
                                                      (   low    )
```

sense of the first facet, where "low" means either "high negative" (if "direction" selected in the first facet) or "zero" (if "magnitude" is selected in the first facet).

The rationale for this theory and ways of testing it are proposed (Shye, 1975) in terms of respondent's pro and con considerations when engaged in the decision making process of picking up a single answer from a given response scale.

Universe of Discourse and Validity Domain of Theories

Consider again the rat behavior experiment illustrated in Chapter 5 and pose the question, What is really being studied here? First, the design is restricted to behavior in a maze. Then, it looks at appetitive behavior of rats toward the goal box. Assessments to this end could be running speed, latency of response, crossing electrical grids that are charged differently, and so forth. What, then, do the items $(d,h,i) \rightarrow r$ measure?

By the definitions in Chapter 7, these items are attitude items. In practice, they are restricted to one particular modality of attitudinal behavior, that is, the instrumental one. It is posssible the attitude object is the maze's goal box, but this may be too coarsely defined. Rather, the object is what is systematically related to the deprivation—food and water. Hence, the Hull-Spence models represent theories about instrumental attitude behavior of rats in mazes toward food and water.

We express this in such a strong form to make a general point. Hull (1952) generalized, without restriction, the findings from such rat studies to a "theory of behavior," not just a "theory of instrumental attitudinal behavior of rats . . ." Such undisciplined generalizations are not uncommon in much of psychology. It always seems better in the long run to discriminate carefully the universe of items (universe of discourse) from other domains. One cannot expect that psychological findings and laws hold without restriction. Therefore, carefully characterizing the universe of discourse explicates the domain for which they are supposedly valid. Cumulative theory construction is made difficult if the respective P-, Q- and R-universes (and their facets) are left ill-defined (and ill-structured). Take, for example, the many "decision theories." They are formally developed very well, but often leave open what kinds of choice alternatives are admissible for their formal place holders. Do they include chewing gum as well as cars and life partners?

Criteria of Good Mapping Definitions

Whether a mapping definition is good or bad must be decided by the same criteria that one uses for distinguishing between good or bad facets (see Chapter 5). That is, a good mapping definition must be semantically clear and conceptually and empirically useful. Thus social psychologists should, for example, be able to use our attitude definition reliably as a decision rule for determining whether a given item is an attitude item. Moreover, Guttman (1982e) stated that

definitions without hypotheses in mind may merely lead to sterility. Mathematicians propose definitions to facilitate theorems they have in mind. Mendeleef's classification of elements had various uniformities of compounds in mind. Our definition of attitude had the First Law of Attitude and further faceted laws in mind. (p. 57)

Items that satisfy the attitude item definition given in Chapter 7 (together with a number of side constraints discussed in the first section of this chapter) can be reasonably hypothesized to correlate positively among each other (the First Law of Attitude). This is certainly not so for any items. The lawfulness does not make our definition for attitude items less arbitrary than it is, but it suggests not to give it up without good reasons.

In practice, it should not be expected that a good mapping definition is easy to formulate. Typically, one does not start out with a clear-cut definition and then finds a law pertaining to it. In intelligence research, for example, just the opposite was true: it had been known for a long time that intelligence items correlate positively with each other. After many unsuccessful attempts to explain this phenomenon by various "models" (see Schönemann, 1981), Guttman (1965a) essentially brought up the idea to search less for parameters and rules that lie "behind" intelligence behavior but rather for a distinction of intelligence items from other items. He thus concentrated on what these tests have in common. After it was spelled out, their common range became "obvious."

Mapping Definitions and Empirical Implications

Mapping definitions that participate in the formulation of empirical laws are especially valuable. If we succeed to prove that particular items we are interested in satisfy the definition of attitude items, we can immediately assume that they have all the properties of attitude items. It is, therefore, generally worthwhile to check carefully if given items are possibly special cases of a well-understood class of items—just as mathematicians try to trace back a particular problem to something already known.

Assume we are interested in values. The literature abounds with definitions for this notion. Most of them are nominal ones (A value is a judgment . . .). In contrast, a mapping definition could be set up as follows:

> An item belongs to the universe of value items if and only if its domain asks for a {cognitive} assessment of the importance of a {situational, behavioral} goal in a {cognitive, affective, instrumental} modality in life area {x} for {itself as a, a more primary} purpose in life area {y} and the range is ordered from {very important that it should . . . very important that it should not} exist for that purpose. (Levy, 1986, p. 5)

Value items, according to this definition, ask how important it should be that a certain goal is reached or prevented for the sake of a particular purpose (endorsed by the respondent). This corresponds to the philosophical tradition that considers values as norms. Other scholars, in contrast, denote value by the worth, importance, or desirability that an object or its attributes possess as such or for bringing about a desired state of affairs (Fishburn, 1964, 1970; Vroom, 1964). Yet good mapping definitions are usually easy to generalize or modify. In the given case, we can combine both notions of value into a common definition by replacing *should* in Guttman's definition by the facet {*should, does*}. Should, then, expresses the normative notion of value; does, the instrumental one.

In practice, it is common to collect data on values by items that ask the respondent to assess how important certain things such as money, family, status, and so forth are to him or her personally. A purpose is almost never spelled out. To understand such questions, one could argue that the implied purpose is the respondent's personal well-being, so that he or she really answers the question, How important is *X* for your well-being? This still leaves open whether his or her answer is meant in a normative or in an instrumental sense. For example, the respondent might think that money *is* important for well-being, but does not feel that this is the way it *should* be.

One may feel that such considerations are exaggerated and only cause confusion. However, the simple How important? questions look simpler than they are and not pursuing such analyses is likely to slow down theoretical progress in the end. Moreover, better items can only be constructed if one explicates previously uncontrolled facets.

What is particularly important is that value items of the *should* variety are special cases of attitude items, because they assess (cognitive) behavior of a person toward an object in a positive-negative sense. If a person feels that it should be important to reach or avoid a particular goal for some desirable purpose, then he or she has a positive attitude toward reaching or avoiding that goal. The law of attitude monotonicity, then, can be expected to hold for such value items as well. Indeed, there are numerous empirical investigations that confirm this hypothesis (Borg, 1986a; Borg & Galinat, 1986; Elizur, 1984; Levy, 1984, 1986; Levy & Guttman, 1981).

It is not always easy to decide whether given items belong to a particular universe of items. Westhoff (1987) proposed a "first law of concentration," which predicts that "any two tests of concentration . . . from the universe of concentration tests [are monotonically related to each other]" (p. 49). A precise definition of concentration tests is not given. However, Westhoff adds that "because everybody can do every item in every concentration test correctly, it is the speed with which it is done that is the important factor" (p. 52). Westhoff and Kluck (1984) and Westhoff and Lemme (1988) add additional characteristics: (a) the testee must be "highly motivated" and (b) the test items must be easy. It is clear that these additional restrictions are meant to distinguish among causes for bad performance and, consequently, concentration disability from, say, poor intelligence. Yet as definitional criteria of concentration behavior they are problematic because, strictly speaking, they depend on measures of ease and motivation that must be empirically determined.

In any case, the law of concentration considers tests rather than test items. (Such items ask the testee, for example, to cancel letters printed on paper if and only if they are As.) At first glance it would seem that it is not more correct to do something more quickly and that the speed range is not a variant of the right-wrong range of intelligence items. However, the question of how long does it take the testee to come up with the right answer to an item can be recast into a series of items of the form: Did the testee come up with the right answer within 2 seconds? . . . within 3 seconds? . . . within n seconds? (see also Guttman, 1992). Hence, the reaction time can be incorporated into the observational design as a content facet (rather than as a range facet). Viewed in this way, it becomes clear that concentration items are a special case of intelligence items.

Item Batteries and Rules for Culling Items Versus Item Analysis

In practical research, one can distinguish three approaches to constructing item batteries: (a) An exploratory one in which item batteries are more or less given and empirical research is done to clarify the items' content, (b) a traditional item-analytic approach in which one starts out with a vague notion of commonality for formulating or culling items and then proceeds to purify the set of items by statistical analysis of observations on these items, and (c) a deductive approach in which an item universe is defined a priori and data are used to study the empirical structure of items in this universe.

The Exploratory Approach

To illustrate the first approach, consider Schuessler's well-known scales on social life feelings (Schuessler, 1982). They were derived (Krebs & Schuessler, 1987) from variables that represented

the result of social science efforts to assess individual and collective responses to structurally induced difficult life situations and, as such, constitute the subjective reflections of societal-structural circumstances [to allow for an] accumulation of experiences and insights rather than a never ending repetition of constructing measurement instruments. (p. 2)

Schuessler (1982) started out with a set of 1800 items—selected "on somewhat arbitrary decisions" from the sociological literature (p. 143)—which was reduced by content considerations and pretests to 14 topics with 237 items. Data were collected on these items and 120 items were extracted by factor analytic methods to form the final social life feelings (SLF) scales. The question of what the remaining items actually assess is answered only afterward. Indeed, "the concept social life feeling . . . is the common denominator . . . [and] was adopted in the course of constructing the scales, not beforehand" (Schuessler, 1982, p. ix).

Such exploratory approaches are sometimes useful, and there are no logical reasons that exclude a posteriori substantive insights. The "operationalizations" for social feelings given by Krebs and Schuessler (1987) specify that the items are "on the one hand judgments on social circumstances, on the functioning of the social world and social life, and on the other affective responses to these circumstances" (pp. 1-2). Thus we have the distinction of an affective and a cognitive behavior modality for the domain of SLF items. The instrumental modality, how one assesses what the person does or intends to do in response to these circumstances, is not addressed.

The range of SLF items remains unspecified. In checking Schuessler's items, several ranges are evident. Some cases have the range that is characteristic for attitude items, with social circumstances as attitude objects. Other cases have other ranges and other Q-facets so that one must conclude that there is little reason for combining all 120 SLF items under one common concept.

A general problem of the exploratory approach is that it mixes substantive and data analytic procedures. The remaining SLF items are partially the result of a statistical filtering process that forces certain formal properties onto the item battery without paying attention to contents. The formal properties are not even substantively motivated but, as is true in factor analysis, represent notions that were separated from their original function as models for certain contents (see, e.g., Schönemann, 1981) and that now drift around in the conceptual space as "portable theories" (Coombs, 1983).

The Item Analysis Approach

A completely exploratory approach is, however, never used in practice. This is also true in Schuessler's (1982) example, in which he acknowledges having "somewhat arbitrary," criteria for the initial selection of items. The common approach to set up item batteries puts more emphasis on setting up a priori notions on the content of the items. If one were to construct, for example, an intelligence test along the lines of "item analysis," one would first collect items that supposedly measure intelligence into a comprehensive item pool. Then, this pool is studied empirically and reduced by eliminating items that do not satisfy statistical criteria such as factorial homogeneity. What remains in the item battery is forced into a preconceived formal structure, or, in other words, only items with certain statistical properties classify in the end as intelligence items. Therefore, one might say that certain items that were initially considered intelligence items are later on—on the basis of empirical data and formal properties—classified as nonintelligence items. If this decision is not motivated by applied considerations (one wants an economical item battery) or model-related theory (as in Thurstone's, 1935, simple structure notion, for example), then it essentially expresses the fallacious belief that content can be derived from statistical properties (see Chapter 4 for a counter-example).

The FT Approach: Separating Definitions From Empirical Structures

In FT, setting up an item battery is typically done by first defining the characteristics for a particular item universe. This involves defining the range and possibly some content facets. Items are then either constructed according to these criteria or culled from existing sets of items.

A purely deductive approach would, however, be too restrictive if one wants to take maximal advantage of available data. If such data are there, then it often pays to start out with a preliminary item definition, which is then differentiated and possibly extended to cover more content and more items. As an example, consider the SLF items once more. Borg and Staufenbiel (1993) wanted to show that the SLF scales contain another, more meaningful structure than just factors. Because of its interesting content, they first turned their attention to the SLF-S6 scale, "future outlook," which assesses the respondent's expectations about future events. Two of its items are: "The future of this country looks very uncertain"; and "Although things keep changing all the time, one still knows what to expect from one day to the next." One notes that, with certain interpretations, the first item is an attitude item and the second is not. Only attitude items were selected from the SLF-S6 because of their commonality with respect to the meaning of the range.

The object of the attitudinal behavior can be defined to be an aspect of the respondent's future environment. This immediately suggests two Q-facets: (a) Instead of just future we can use point in time = {past, present, future}; and (b) environment can be faceted into {primary, secondary} environment or, even finer, as in Chapter 5, into {internal self, self in interaction with other persons, country, mankind}. The environment facet is ordered from *very central* to *very peripheral* for the person.

Facets that proved successful in past research—such as the environment facet—are often good candidates for new studies. Thus, life areas also could be considered here, but there was not enough systematic variation in the existing SLF items in this respect. Yet the items addressed another facet that is even more useful in general, the modality of the attitudinal behavior. This led to a third facet: {cognitive, affective} behavior. So we have the following mapping sentence:

```
                                      (   a = affective   )
        Respondent (r) assesses in an (                   )   modality
                                      (   c = cognitive   )


                                      (   s = primary             )
        (   an aspect of his/her  )   (   i = primary interaction )   (social) environment
                                      (   c = secondary-country   )
                                      (   w = secondary-world     )


                   (   1 = past     )            (   very positive )
        vis-à-vis  (   2 = present  )   →        (   . . .         )
                   (   3 = future   )            (   very negative )
```

TABLE 7.1 Twenty-Three Items That Assess Attitudes on One's Social Life[a]

No	short	Struct.	M	Question of Item
1	trust	(c,I,2)	.64	It is hard to figure out who you can really trust these days.
2	more unempl.	(c,M,3)	.75	More people will be out of work in the next few years.
3	future bleak	(a,S,3)	.46	The future looks very bleak.
4	country sick	(c,C,2)	.43	In my opinion, this country is sick.
5	lose freedom	(c,C,3)	.65	We are slowly losing our freedom to the government.
6	world up	(c,M,3)	.63	Taking everything into account, the world is getting better.
7	get worse	(c,C,3)	.53	The lot of the average man is getting worse, not better.
8	child unfair	(c,I,3)	.35	It's unfair to bring children into the world with the way things look for the future.
9	values down	(c,M,3)	.77	Many things our parents stood for are going down the drain.
10	friends gone	(a,I,1)	.24	I sometimes feel forgotten by friends.
11	life useless	(a,I,2)	.21	I just can't help feeling that my life is not very useful.
12	no optimism	(a,S,3)	.35	I find it hard to be optimistic about anything anymore.
13	hard past	(a,S,1)	.41	I've had more than my share of troubles.
14	child happy	(a,S,1)	.29	I was happier as a child than I am now.
15	older = better	(c,S,2)	.31	Things get better for me as I get older.
16	blew chances	(a,S,1)	.48	I regret having missed so many chances in the past.
17	not happier	(a,S,2)	.42	I couldn't be much happier.
18	no confid.	(c,L,3)	.58	I have little confidence in the government today.
19	fut. bright	(a,S,3)	.40	The future looks very bright to me.
20	plans work	(c,I,2)	.20	When I make plans, I am almost certain that I can make them work.
21	much fun	(a,S,1)	.16	I get a lot of fun out of life.
22	much purpose	(c,I,2)	.20	There is much purpose to what I am doing at present.
23	gen. satisf.	(a,S,2)	.22	I am satisfied with the way things are working out for me.

SOURCE: Schuessler (1982).
NOTES: a. The facets are modality = {a = affective, c = cognitive}, centrality of environment = {S = self, I = interaction, C = country, M = mankind} and time-perspective = {1 = past, 2 = present, 3 = future}. The mean in first row is from U.S.-data; a high scores indicates a more negative attitude.

This mapping sentence was used to filter all SLF items and 23 were found to satisfy it. They are shown in Table 7.1 together with their structuples and empirical mean values. To see how the structuple assignments were made here, look at two examples. Items 9 and 18 are both classified as future-related, because they address reduced life perspectives and are thus forward-looking. Item 22 was coded as cognitive, because "seeing much purpose in what one is doing" refers more to a standard of right-wrong rather than to pleasant-unpleasant.

We note in passing that we used the same structuples for both the English and the German versions of the SLF items, even though one can question in some cases if the different languages always stress the same facets equally. More generally, this shows how useful it is for cross-cultural research to work with items for which such a common definitional system exists. Such a system makes the translations much easier and reliable, because they make clear what the essential semantic features of the items are (Borg, 1993a).

Table 7.1, then, provides a set of items, culled from various SLF scales on the basis of a mapping sentence. The semantic content of these items is sufficiently clear. Our definitions, obviously, were not dependent on observations about these data or even on using particular statistical methodology such as factor analysis. (In Chapter 11, we will see how the data are structured and whether our definitional system corresponds to the data structure in some way.)

Note

1. Often, these and other terms are interchanged for stylistic reasons. We prefer to define a term and then use this term as often as needed. One could even argue that a dry but precise language is typical for particularly successful sciences. No one in mathematics, for example, feels compelled to replace the term + by variant terms such as *and, plus* and so forth, even if it appears dozens of times on one page.

General Principles of Correspondence
of Design and Data

- Principle of Empirical Nontriviality
- Principle of Formal Control of Variance
- Principle of Discriminability
- Contiguity Principle

Even though definitions are arbitrary, one can still distinguish between good and bad ones. Truth is not the criterion. Rather, it is clarity of semantics, reliability for classifications, and usefulness for constructing a theory in a domain of interest. A good definition serves to clearly distinguish the universe of discourse from other universes. Moreover, it helps to set up a conceptual structure that allows one to classify, cull, and construct items. It also leads to mapping sentences that serve as springboards for fruitful extension and further differentiation. Ultimately, however, the worth of a definition depends on its "partnership" with empirical phenomena, constituting a lawful correspondence between the definition and a well-defined aspect (statistic) of the data.

This general hypothesis of FT comes in many forms. It is not confined to particular statistics or data analytical models such as correlation coefficients or multidimensional scaling, for example. The following examines a number of such correspondences between definitional systems and data. First some general principles are reviewed, followed by an examination of more specialized hypotheses. These are more powerful in practice, but often require particular data analytical methods.

Principle of Empirical Nontriviality

As the most general hypothesis on the correspondence of definitions and data, one can require that the definitions should be linked to some regularity in empirical data. That is to say that if the definitions are satisfied, then certain empirical relations are also true, provided a number of conditions are satisfied. The relations, of course, must not be logically implied by the definitions or the constraints, for otherwise there is nothing to demonstrate empirically. If one finds this if-then combination of definitions, side constraints, and empirical relations true repeatedly and without exception, one calls it an *empirical law.*

Many laws have been found within the FT approach. A prominent example is the law of intelligence monotonicity: Items that satisfy the definitional criteria for intelligence items always satisfy this law (given the side constraints). For other items, this law need not be expected to hold (see Chapter 9).

The clearer the definitional system is explicated—that is, the more it is expressed in technical or even formal language—the easier it is to test the law and to find out under exactly what definitions and what side constraints one can expect to reliably find an empirical regularity.

The principle of empirical nontriviality is really quite demanding because it requires one to show that one can, for some data, not only explain some dependent variables with some independent variables, but also puts particular emphasis on replicability and precisely explicated definitions of premises and side constraints. There is no scientific reason for holding onto definitional systems that do not prove empirically useful, even if they are conceptually clear and intuitively plausible.

Principle of Formal Control of Variance

Expressed in traditional terms, one hypothesizes for a definitional system that its facets allow one to explain variance in the data. This is most obvious in experimental design that is typically and intimately related to ANOVA methods. ANOVA asks whether the facets have an "effect" on the data and checks how large such effects are relative to variance that remains uncontrolled or unaccounted (error).

For the duration judgments in Chapter 1, a factorial ANOVA shows that the content facets indeed have such effects (Galinat & Borg, 1987). ANOVA, however, is quite restrictive (linear combination of interval scaled data). It admits, in particular, interaction terms that are often nothing more than "formal noise," which reflect a poor understanding of the roles of the facets relative to the data (see Luce, 1989).

It is possible, though, to minimize the interaction terms via conjoint measurement (Krantz, Luce, Suppes, & Tversky, 1971). An alternative route is to simply drop them in the statistical model. That is what Rossi (1982) and his colleagues do in their factorial survey approach, in which they use multiple regression without interaction terms for predicting the respondents' judgments from the facets (see Chapter 4).

Many other statistical composition rules of population and content facets are possible when it comes to statistically explaining the observations. Whatever the rule, however, one always looks for a correspondence of design and data by attempting to approximate the data or account for the data by facets of the design—that is, regress the data onto the facets.

Principle of Discriminability

The above regression principle can be complemented by a *discrimination* principle. Most research uses stimuli and persons that are facetized into classes. We can ask whether these classes of the observational domain—that is, the different questions or person types, or both—are somehow preserved in the observational mapping.

The general principle of discriminability then says that the distinctions made by facets on P or Q should be reflected in corresponding differences in the data. We saw one typical application of this principle in Chapter 1, in which three of the four facets of the questions could be used to partition a geometric representation of the item intercorrelations such that each region of this partition corresponded to exactly one struct of a selected facet (Figures 1.4 through 1.6).

This type of regional correspondence of design and data has been found to be most successful in empirical applications. Nothing guarantees, of course, that definitional system and data are related in this way. The respondent typically is not aware of the facets used to structure the questions. But even if the facets are obvious or are put forward in an obtrusive way—as in factorial surveys or in paper-and-pencil applications of conjoint measurement—the person responds to a complete question as a "commodity bundle" and not to particular structs separately. Consequently, finding empirical discriminability for a definitional system is a remarkable nontrivial correspondence.

Contiguity Principle

A predecessor of the above principles is the contiguity principle (Foa, 1958; Guttman, 1959b; Runkel & MacGrath, 1968). This principle is often incorrectly believed to be "the basic theorem of facet analysis" (Wagner, Huerkamp, Jockisch, & Graumann, 1990) or viewed as FT's "central proposition . . . [and] absolutely critical assumption" (Brown, 1985, p. 20).

The contiguity principle is based on the seemingly plausible idea that "variables which are more similar in their facet structure will also be more related empirically" (Foa, 1965, p. 264). Similarity in facet structure is typically defined as the number of structs that two structuples have in common, whereas empirical similarity is assessed by some correlation between items (Foa, 1958).

It is not necessary to discuss here whether similarity should be measured in this way or whether one should somehow also weight the differences of corresponding structs (for ordered facets) or use other similarity coefficients for the structuples and data. Such refinements cannot save the contiguity principle in the above form: From the formal similarity of structuples generally nothing can be predicted about the empirical similarity of the respective items. One example makes this clear.

Look at two mapping sentences, M1 and M2:

M1: The preference strength of (p) for . . .

M2: The estimate of (p) concerning the assets of . . .

	(	large	)		(	conservative	)			(	great	)
. . .a	(		)	and	(		)	party	$\rightarrow$	(	. . .	)
	(	small	)		(	liberal	)			(	small	)

M1 and M2 have the same content facets—{large, small} and {conservative, liberal}—but they ask different questions. Indeed, it is quite plausible that respondents may base their preferences primarily on the distinction conservative-liberal, whereas the parties' size determines their estimated assets.

The content facets give rise to four types of parties: a = (large, conservative); b = (large, liberal); c = (small, conservative); and d = (small, liberal). By simply counting common elements in pairs of structuples, one derives a circular order of contiguity for a, b, c and d, because a and b have one element in common, a and c none, and so forth. Obviously, this kind of analysis does not provide sufficient reason for predicting a corresponding circular order of similarity for questions such as those asked in M1 or M2 nor, a fortiori, for answers to these questions.

Attempts to amend this situation by weighting the facets (Foa, 1965) are also doomed to fail as long as the range is ignored. What is required, in contrast, is to analyze the relation of each facet to the particular range. Only if each facet is ordered, and ordered in the same sense relative to the range, can the contiguity principle be saved in principle. However, even then, the question remains how one could justify a universal equal weighting of the different facets. Hence, in most cases, partial order hypotheses seem to be the most for which one can hope.

Bivariate Regression Hypotheses

- Monotonicity Hypotheses (Sign Hypotheses)
- Laws of Polytonicity (Regression Hypotheses for Different Item Universes)

Meta principles for the correspondence of design and data are usually too general for practical theory construction. We, therefore, look at more specialized types of hypotheses. There exist several such types, differing in various respects among each other: Some constitute systems of hypotheses with many variants (regional hypotheses), others are much more specialized (scalability hypotheses); some are quite restrictive (metric radex), others are softer (partitionability); some require particular computerized data analysis procedures (SSA, MSA, POSAC), others can be checked with paper and pencil (simple partial orders).

We will point out such distinctions in the following whenever they are useful for the applied researcher. Otherwise, we organize the special correspondence hypotheses into three classes: (a) bivariate regression hypotheses for item universes, (b) hypotheses on the correspondence between content (or, range) facets and patterns of data (or, content) structuples, and (c) hypotheses on the correspondence of content facets to similarity structures in the data.

Monotonicity Hypotheses (Sign Hypotheses)

Monotonicity hypotheses predict that the observations for every two items in a given content universe with a common range are monotonically related. The items should therefore correlate nonnegatively among each other. This is sometimes called a sign hypothesis, because all interitem correlations—except those that are exactly equal to zero—are predicted to have a positive sign. Sign hypotheses that have been shown to hold empirically in many independent studies are also called laws of monotonicity (or first laws). The following examines two particularly famous examples.

The Law of Attitude Monotonicity

Formally, the attitude of a person p toward an object o is assessed by item i's mapping of p onto an element of the range {very positive, . . . , very negative} behavior toward object o. Each item i refers to a particular behavior of p toward o. Therefore, there are infinitely many attitudes of p toward o, one for each item i.

The law of attitude monotonicity, then, states that in the population (of persons) each pair of attitude items toward the same object are positively correlated. Guttman (1978), who formulated this law, adds these comments:

The idea of the First Law was suggested by seeing an empirical feature of the data recurring in many different contexts of research over the past forty years: correlation coefficients among certain items (which were informally classified as attitudinal) were always positive. A parallel phenomenon was known for over eighty years for intelligence test items. Implicit acknowledgement of the attitudinal Law is made by the widespread—and anti-theoretical—practice of "item analysis": practitioners simply throw out items which empirically do not show the anticipated positive correlations. To define and establish the First Law of Attitude requires doing just the opposite of common practice. Definition of whether or not an item belongs to the universe of variables must be made independently of the observations. The sign of the correlation coefficient is then an empirically testable hypothesis. If the hypothesis turns out to be wrong, then it is the hypothesis that is to be rejected not the items. . . . The hypothesis is, that when all . . . conditions are satisfied, then the phenomenon of positive correlations should occur. This *hypothesis* has become elevated to the status of law by virtue of the standard scientific procedure of having it verified over and over again in a broad spectrum of circumstances. . . . The First Law . . . is for a population as a whole, not for individuals. Any correlation that is not precisely equal to +1 implies that there are individuals who are "contradictory" in their behavior. The Law refers to the overall trend within the population as a whole. . . . Special cases of attitudinal behavior that have been formally distinguished include: values, adjustive behavior (including well-being and coping), worries, protest. The First Law of Attitude holds for each of these. Values concerning the same object are all positively correlated, adjustive behaviors of self toward the same situation are all positively intercorrelated, etc. (pp. 5-7)

The law of attitude monotonicity is expected to hold under the following conditions: (a) All items are attitude items, according to the mapping definition given in Chapter 7, (b) all items refer to the same attitude object, (c) the population of persons is not artificially selected with respect to the attitude object.

The third condition, in particular, is vague and surely needs more research. It is meant to express a condition that is illustrated by the following example. Assume we want to assess attitudes toward the church. If we only ask priests, then we have an artificially selected population, because priests most likely have such similar attitudes toward the church that this essentially eliminates the most important source of variance for the first law of attitudes—that is, the attitude object. The effects of such systematic selection errors on correlations are known from statistics.

A different perspective on the issue of "natural" populations is provided by Shye (1985b) by considering partial-order generated distributions (p. 111). He proved a theorem that for partial order scalograms whose dimensions are independent, the correlation between every pair of items must be nonnegative.

Concerning the object in Condition 2, Levy (1981) suggested distinguishing whether the items ask about complementary or competing aspects of an object: The law, then, is predicted to hold only for complementary aspects. Expressed differently, if the items address competing aspects of an object, then they are actually referring to a different attitude objects—for example, hot tea and iced tea instead of tea in general.

In any case, one notes that these conditions are but starting points and not the final answer. To make them more precise requires further research and, in fact, traces out avenues for doing cumulative theory construction.

It is interesting to look briefly at suggestions similar to the First Law of Attitudes in the literature. Green (1954), for example, defined an attitude as a disposition inferred from the "consistency among responses to a specified set of stimuli, or social objects" (p. 335). The problem of such a definition, however, is that it is actually a hypothesis. It elevates certain empirical observations to definitional criteria and eliminates them from further empirical research. The central notion of *responses,* on the other hand, is not defined any further.

The Law of Intelligence Monotonicity

Much older and at least as well established as the First Law of Attitudes is the first law of intelligence. It has been known for some time that intelligence items usually correlate positively among each other. Spearman

(1927) and Thurstone (1935), among others, tried, without success, to explain this fact using models that specify how the answers on intelligence tasks are generated from a set of underlying parameters (Schönemann, 1981). A definition for intelligence items, however, was not given, and, therefore, the empirical law as such is left rather ambiguous, because without specifying the domain for which it is supposed to hold, one cannot really test a law.

Note here that such definitions are sometimes misunderstood as mere descriptions of reality. Actually, they are necessary conditions for formulating testable laws. It also is not true that models such as those by Spearman or Thurstone represent "deeper" scientific efforts, because they ask for what lies "behind" the phenomena. Taking a closer look, one finds that such latent factors are indeed closely linked to the items' domain facets (see Chapter 11).

The conditions of the law of intelligence monotonicity are (as of today): (a) All items are intelligence items, according to the mapping definition in Chapter 7 and (b) the population is not artificially selected (Guttman, in Gratch, 1973, p. 37) in the sense that the persons have a particular relation to the items.

Condition 2, obviously, is quite similar—also in its vagueness—to Condition 3 for the First Law of Attitudes. Shye (1978d) commented on this as follows:

> Once stated, the first law of intelligence invites scientists to test its applicability in diverse contexts to find and characterize situations where the law does not hold. Such "failures" can lead to constructive sharpening . . . of the definitional framework—for example, by clarifying what constitutes a "nonartificial" or a natural population in the context of intelligence testing or possibly by further restricting the definition of intelligence items. (p. 18)

Laws of Polytonicity
(Regression Hypotheses for Different Item Universes)

The law of attitude monotonicity requires that all items have a common attitude object and a common range. If the second condition is dropped, then there are items from different universes. There is generally *no* reason to expect these items to correlate positively among each other.

The ranges of such items may, however, correspond to those of the principal components of attitudes, provided they assess the person's behavior toward the object in toward-away, strong-weak, and so forth, terms and provided that these behaviors are all related to a constant object (see Chapter 7). If this is so, then one can predict particular regression curves for items from different components. That is, we should expect U-, N- and M-shaped curves, as discussed in Chapter 7. For items that relate all to the same component, there may be reason to hypothesize a corresponding law of monotonicity.

10 Hypotheses for Structuples

- Qualitative Facets and Multidimensional Structuple Analysis

- Ordered Facets and Partial Order Structuple Analysis (POSA)

We now look at some hypotheses and procedures that concern correspondences of facets on P and Q to empirical profiles. An empirical profile is simply the vector of answers that a person gives to a battery of items. This usually corresponds to a row in the person-by-items data matrix. Guttman (1991) called such profiles *structuples,* just as the structuples we considered above—that is, elements of Cartesian products of facets. Empirical profiles are indeed structuples in this sense, because the person-by-items matrix is just a short-hand form of expressing a categorical mapping of the domain P onto the Cartesian product of the range facets. Using the term *structuple* (or, rather, *data structuple* to distinguish this type of structuple from the *content structuple* considered above) allows a unified treatment of such objects, irrespective of how they originate.

Qualitative Facets and Multidimensional Structuple Analysis

Assume we have only nominal range facets. That is to say, we assign a qualitative role to the facets (Velleman & Wilkinson, 1993). It does not mean that the facets are inherently nominal, or that they are assumed to be nominal. Role assignments are made with a particular hypothesis in mind. For qualitative range facets, this hypothesis is that there is a correspondence between the distinctions made by the facets and certain classes of the structuples. Such hypotheses can be formulated and studied differ-

TABLE 10.1 Eight Hypothetical Structuples With Four Facets

	Facets			
Structuple	F1	F2	F3	F4
A	2	1	1	1
B	3	2	1	1
C	3	2	2	1
D	3	2	2	2
E	2	3	2	2
F	1	3	2	2
G	1	1	2	2
H	1	1	1	1

ently—for example, in a univariate (e.g., marginal distributions; Guttman, 1988; Guttman et al., 1988), bivariate (e.g., contingency tables) or multivariate manner. The following addresses the multivariate case.

Principles of MSA

Basic Concepts

The particular perspective through which nominal data structuples will be addressed is the data analytic method multidimensional structuple analysis (MSA). MSA was originally coined as "multidimensional scalogram analysis" (Lingoes, 1968, 1973; Zvulun, 1978) and later renamed to "multidimensional structuple analysis" (Guttman, 1985c). It attempts to represent structuples as points in a multidimensional space so that the space can be partitioned, facet by facet, into regions that contain only points with the same struct. In general, this is possible only if the data have a particular structure.

Consider the data matrix in Table 10.1. Each structuple (row) of this table can be regarded as a cell in a four-way cross-tabulation, or as a point in a four-dimensional space. The four coordinates serve as the coordinates of this space. The order of the categories within each facet (column) of Table 10.1 is arbitrary, and so the four-dimensional representation is not unique. "Regardless," as Guttman (1985c) states

> it has no special scientific merit. The task set by MSA is to see whether an equivalent representation can be made in a low-dimensional space, subject to the restriction called *regionality*. Each structuple again is to appear as a cell (or point) in the low-dimensional space, but in such a way—that for each

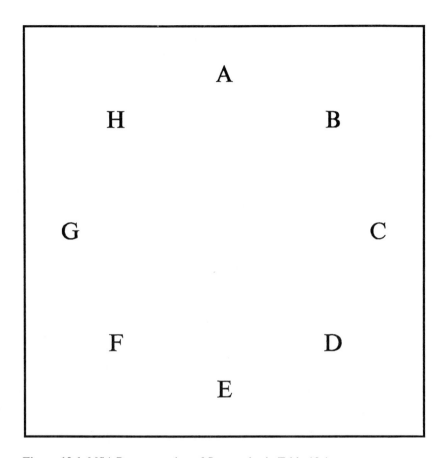

Figure 10.1. MSA Representation of Structuples in Table 10.1

criterion—all structuples which are the same on the criterion (have the same struct) shall be contiguous with each other. Thus, each criterion should correspond to a partition of the space into contiguous regions, one region for each category and criterion. The cell of a structuple as a whole, then, is the intersection of its structs. The lowest dimensionality is sought that will enable such regional contiguity for all the criteria simultaneously. If success is achieved with small dimensionality, the regionality structure tends to be unique and meaningful. (p. 49)

Figure 10.1 shows an MSA representation for the structuples (rows) of Table 10.1. The structuples A, . . . , H—in practice typically data structuples

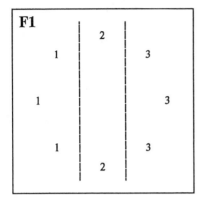

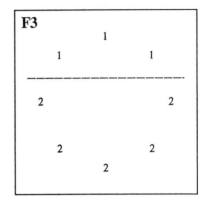

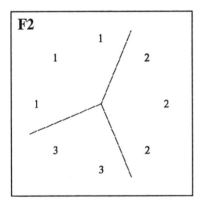

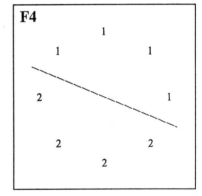

Figure 10.2. Facet Diagrams Over the MSA Representation in Figure 10.1
NOTE: F1 through F4 are the facets in Table 10.1.

for different persons—are represented here in a two-dimensional space
(plane). Figure 10.2 demonstrates by facet diagrams why this configuration is a solution to the MSA problem: Each item, through its respective
range facet (F1, . . . , F4), allows a partition of the space subject to the
condition that the points that represent structuples, which, on facet Fi, have
the same element, occupy a distinct region. This condition should hold for
each of the four facets. MSA maps structuples into points, facet elements
into regions, and facets into partitions of the space.

The correspondence hypothesis, then, is that each facet partitions the MSA space perfectly. This becomes nontrivial if the dimensionality of the space is "low" relative to the number of points. To see why MSA partitionability is a remarkable finding, assume that we write the structuples of Table 10.1 on eight ping-pong balls. We throw these balls into a bucket, mix them thoroughly, and then pour this bucket out onto a billiards table. Once the balls come to a resting position, we try to partition this configuration by each facet in turn. Clearly, this should be difficult, in general, and it becomes a lot more difficult when (a) the number of ping-pong balls or (b) the number of facet elements goes up or both, or (c) we insist on "simple" partitions such as straight lines or all three of the above conditions. Moreover, if such partitions are successful, the question arises—as in all empirical research—(d) whether this structure is replicated in repeated experiments of the same sort.

About MSA Algorithms

MSA attempts to represent structuples as points in a geometric space such that (a) the space can be partitioned by each and every facet of the structuples and (b) the solution is attained in a space of small dimensionality.

There are several algorithms and programs for MSA (Lingoes, 1968, 1973). They differ in the scale level they assign to the facets and in the shape they impose on the partition lines. MSA-I is the most general: It only assumes nominal facets and leaves the shape of the partition lines indefinite. MSA-II assumes that all items have the same range and constrains the partition lines to circles. MSA-III constrains the partition lines, item by item, to be straight and parallel.

The algorithm of MSA-I, probably the best known procedure in this family, is based on the notion of *outer-* and *inner-points*. Given a particular (trial) distribution of points, let us focus our attention on one facet of the structuples, X, and on one of its elements, x_i. We determine the boundary of the region of the points that belong to x_i by identifying its outer-points: For every point that does not belong to x_i, there exists a closest point that does belong to x_i; such a point is an outer point of x_i. All points that are not outer points of x_i are inner-points of x_i. The set of all points belonging to a given x_i is said to occupy a *contiguous* region if each of x_i's inner-points is closer to some outer-point of x_i than it is to an outer-point of any other element of Facet X.

Lingoes (1979, 1981) described some variants of this definition of contiguity by way of the following definitional mapping sentence, in which "exterior" points denote the vertices of a convex polyhydral hull that envelops the points in R:

		(inner-point)		
		(outer-point)		(some)
A region R is contiguous if (each)		(point)	of R is closer to	( )
		(centroid)		(all)
		(exterior point)		

(inner-point)		(inner-point)	
(outer-point)	of R than	(outer-point)	of another region
(points)	it is to any	(points)	R' $(R \neq R')$.
(centroids)		(centroids)	
(exterior points)		(exterior points)	

Within this framework, the definition of contiguity used by MSA-I is, therefore, a relatively weak one. It does not require that the regions be convex, for example. On the other hand, if the distribution of points in space is sparse, then it tends to generate simply connected regions, excluding, for example, regions that form concentric bands as in a circumplex.

In MSA-I, deviations from perfect contiguity are produced by inner-points that are closer to some outer-point of another region than to an outer-point of its own region, facet by facet. For a given MSA-I solution, the *coefficient of contiguity*, λ, ranging from -1 to $+1$ (for perfect contiguity), takes into account the number of deviant points as well as the size of the deviations computed over all facets of all items. For a given dimensionality, MSA-I strives to iteratively maximize this coefficient using a steepest ascent algorithm (Lingoes, 1968). These notions will now be illustrated and extended through an example.

Content Facets in MSA Space

Lewy and Haran (1969) studied patterns of reacting to frustrations of other persons. They considered pity, attempt to help, reproach, withdrawal, disgust, mockery, anger, and malicious joy. Twenty different situations were described: for example, Teacher T. requires discipline from his pupils, but the children are disobedient and he cannot control them. Fifty-six subjects were asked how strongly they would react to such situations with each of these eight behaviors. Their ratings were averaged over the twenty situations. The rounded response scores are shown in Table 10.2. Forty-five different structuples were observed, in which a 5 indicates the strongest reaction.

We now look at these data in terms of MSA. We used MSA-III in the following to generate a first solution and then improved this solution by hand.

TABLE 10.2 Data Structuples Expressing the Likelihood to React to the Frustration of Others[a]

No	1	2	3	4	5	6	7	8	freq
1	1	1	1	1	1	1	1	1	4
2	5	1	1	1	1	4	1	1	3
3	3	1	1	1	1	3	1	1	2
4	2	1	1	1	1	2	1	1	2
5	4	2	1	1	1	3	2	1	2
6	4	1	1	1	1	4	1	1	2
7	4	1	1	1	1	3	1	1	2
8	3	1	1	1	1	2	1	1	2
9	4	2	2	1	1	3	2	2	1
10	3	1	2	1	2	2	1	1	1
11	4	2	2	2	1	3	2	1	1
12	3	1	1	2	2	3	1	1	1
13	4	1	1	1	1	4	1	2	1
14	5	2	2	2	2	5	2	4	1
15	5	3	3	4	3	4	3	4	1
16	1	1	1	1	1	4	1	1	1
17	4	1	1	2	1	2	1	1	1
18	4	2	1	2	1	2	1	3	1
19	3	1	1	1	1	4	1	2	1
20	1	1	1	1	1	2	1	1	1
21	4	2	3	1	2	4	2	2	1
22	4	1	1	2	1	3	1	1	1
23	3	1	2	1	1	4	1	1	1
24	3	2	2	2	2	4	1	4	1
25	3	2	2	2	2	3	2	1	1
26	4	3	3	2	1	5	2	3	1
27	4	2	2	2	2	4	2	2	1
28	4	1	1	1	1	2	1	1	1
29	5	2	1	1	1	4	1	1	1
30	2	1	1	1	1	4	1	3	1
31	2	1	2	1	1	2	1	1	1
32	2	2	1	2	2	1	1	1	1
33	4	2	1	2	1	2	2	2	1
34	5	2	1	1	1	2	1	3	1
35	4	1	2	2	2	3	2	2	1
36	4	2	1	2	2	2	1	2	1
37	3	3	2	2	1	4	2	3	1
38	4	1	2	1	1	4	1	4	1
39	3	1	1	1	1	5	1	4	1
40	3	2	1	1	1	4	1	1	1
41	5	3	2	3	1	4	1	5	1
42	4	3	2	2	1	2	2	1	1
43	2	1	1	2	2	2	2	2	1
44	4	2	2	3	2	3	1	2	1
45	2	1	1	1	1	3	1	1	1

SOURCE: Lewy and Haran (1969).
NOTES: a. *1* = pity, *2* = disgust, *3* = anger, *4* = mockery, *5* = malicious joy, *6* = attempt to help, *7* = withdrawal, *8* = reproach; freq = frequency of structuple.

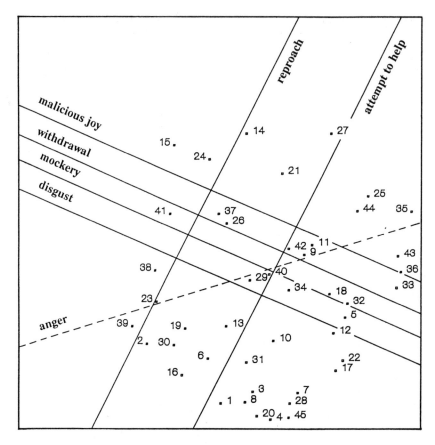

Figure 10.3. MSA Representation of Structuples in Table 10.2, Together With Partition Lines Induced by Seven Facets

Computing MSA solutions is quite difficult, so that optimal solutions cannot be guaranteed. Corrections by hand were done here in order to improve the above criterion of contiguity (partitionability) simultaneously for all facets.

Note that such corrections are not desirable—better algorithms are!— but admissible. Computer solutions are not better just because they come from the computer. Indeed, it is irrelevant how a solution is found.[1] Figure 10.3 is a good solution to the MSA problem and that is easy to verify.

Figure 10.3 shows the improved MSA-III, together with seven partitioning lines that represent seven of the eight items. How the partitioning lines

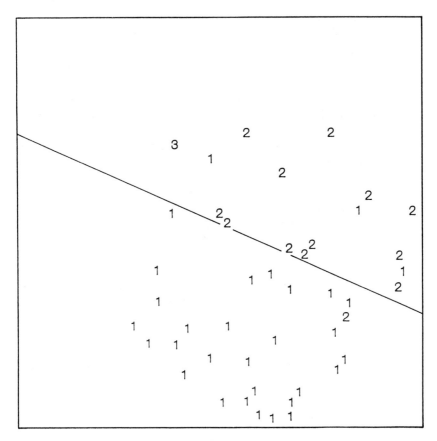

Figure 10.4. Item Diagram Over MSA Representation in Figure 10.3
NOTE: Numbers indicate scores on the item withdrawal.

come about is illustrated in Figure 10.4. This figure is a facet diagram (similar to those in Figure 10.2); it is a copy of the MSA-III solution of Figure 10.3, except that the points representing the structuples are labeled by their scores on the item withdrawal. In case in which the structuples are data structuples, a facet diagram is called item diagram. One notes that, in this diagram, a straight line separates 1s from 2s and 3s, with only a few errors. Similar item diagrams can be drawn for every other item. Except for the item pity, they all lead to partitions with little or no error.

Figure 10.3, then, tells us that the different facets constitute primarily two systems of partitions, creating the checkerboard pattern of a duplex.

This suggests a basic system of two dimensions, such as strength of affect toward the hero on the one side (which ranges from *disgust* to *malicious joy*), to an active-passive distinction of coping with the situation on the other (which ranges from *reproach* to *attempt to help*). In such a system, the various reactions (such as disgust) are regarded as observed manifestations of these two basic dimensions. Anger, of course, does not fit into either dimension but may be a combination of the two. Pity seems to be something completely different.

The dimensions are derived only afterward by thinking further about the items' content: In what sense is reproach stronger than attempt to help for example? Lewy and Haran (1969) make the following comment:

> The results indicated that two dimensions sufficed for the ordering of the reaction profiles. One possible interpretation of these results is that two range facets suffice for the description of the personal styles as measured in this study. (p. 220)

The interpretation suggests that six of the eight unordered reaction types are but compositions of two more abstract facets.

The dimensionlike interlocking of the reaction types also can be seen by other data-analytic means. Cross-tabulating reproach and attempt to help, for example, reveals that 95% of the respondents have scores on attempt to help that are at least as high as those on reproach. Hence, reproach behavior implies attempts to help.

Range Facets in MSA Space

One can replace the points in an MSA space—which usually represent person's response structuples—by the elements of a particular population (range) facet to see if the distinctions on P are reflected in the empirical structure of the structuples. For example, one might wonder whether men and women can be distinguished in this way. Formally, one asks about the relative distribution of M and W points in the MSA space.

To illustrate such a case, consider Figure 10.5. The data here come from Marcus, Hans, Patterson, and Morris's (1983) research project on the influence of in utero opiate exposure on the functioning of children (see Chapter 6). The MSA space represents 45 neonates as points in a plane. The data structuples are based on five items, three motor items (general tonus, motor maturity, tremulousness) and two cognitive items (general irritability, alertness). These items structure the MSA space in a gridlike fashion, similar to Figure 10.3. Marcus et al. (1983) classify the neonates

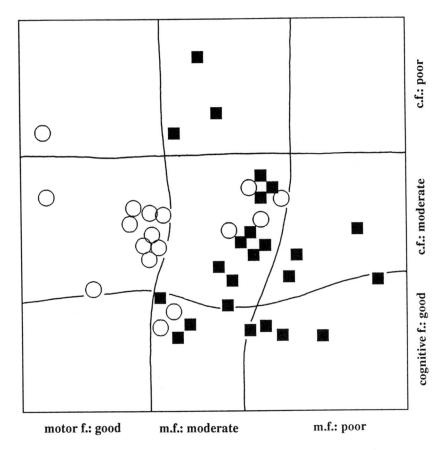

Figure 10.5. MSA Representation of 45 Neonates

NOTE: Representation is based on structuples assessing motor and cognitive functioning. Circles = children with methadone mothers; squares = control mothers.

globally into good, moderate, and poor ones on the basis of their functioning in motor and cognitive behaviors, respectively. This results in nine types, which are reflected in the gridlike partitioning of the MSA space shown in Figure 10.5.

We can now ask if additional information about the neonates that is not contained in the data structuples on which the MSA solution is based will, nevertheless, shed additional light on the MSA point distribution or help in understanding an external variable in terms of the MSA. What was known about the neonates was whether their mother used methadone. This information is represented by the circles (methadone mother) and squares (control group mother). One notes that in the region of the children with poor motor skills, one finds only methadone children; in the region of the children with good motor skills, only control children. Wheras all regions of the cognitive dimension contain both squares and circles. According to Hans et al. (1985),

> the coupling of facet theory with multidimensional analysis of individual profiles produced a finding that was a new contribution to the literature in neuropharmacology: the effects of the withdrawal from methadone on the neonate are not equally observable in all aspects of the central nervous system function. Rather, they are greatest in the motor modality. (p. 169)

At the age of one month, the separation of the methadone children has vanished (Marcus et al., 1983).

Using MSA in Practice

In that, in practice, it is difficult to explore and interpret MSA spaces of dimensionality greater than 2, a two-dimensional solution is usually sought. If the solution is satisfactory (λ close to +1), fine. Otherwise, one breaks up the item set by focusing, in turn, on "cross sections" of Q-facets; that is, on selected structs of Q-facets or, more generally, on selected substruc-tuples of the Q-facets.

Commensurate with its generality is MSA's weakness as a model for substantive theory. Interpretations derive from regularities of the boundaries in MSA space, considered within facets and compared among facets (see, for example, Bloombaum, 1968; Guttman, 1985c; Morrison, 1990; Shalit, 1977; Shoham, Guttman, & Rahav, 1970). MSA, thus, may be useful for dividing the items into different kinds, for seeing structure among the structs, or for collapsing or differentiating structs into more effective categories. MSA solutions, however, are typically quite soft, in particular if the number of different structuples is small. Thus, contrary to many other data analysis techniques, having few cases in MSA would generally ask for many facets in order to stabilize the MSA representation.

Moreover, a second look at the range facets may reveal that they need not be taken as unordered or as not ordered in the same common sense. After some struct rearrangement and reinterpretation, such range facets can often be conceived as ordered with respect to a general concept, however abstract.

Ordered Facets and Partial Order Structuple Analysis (POSA)

Simple Scalability and Partially Ordered Structuple Sets

The classical method for analyzing structuples with a common range is Guttman scaling. In a structuple such as 1101, for example, each 1 indicates more of a common property than 0. If the structuple were based on intelligence items, then a 1 would stand for correct and indicate more intelligence than 0, which would indicate incorrect. If one considers reasonably interesting universes, however, then such (one-dimensional) scalability is almost never a viable hypothesis. Rather, scalability is typically a result the researcher "wants" to obtain (mostly for applied reasons) rather than what can be reasonably predicted. Cliff (1983) writes explicitly that "even with an unsophisticated—but intelligent—consumer of psychometrics, one has only to show him a perfect scale and recognition is almost instantaneous, 'Yes, that's what I want' " (p. 284).

Given that all items share a common range, a partial order, unlike a complete (linear) order, always exists. The difference between a complete order and a partial order is that in the latter not all elements are comparable. Consider the data structuples[2] $A = (1,1)$, $B = (0,1)$, $C = (1,0)$, and $D = (0,0)$. Assume that there is a common range on all facets so that $0 < 1$ in the same sense everywhere. Then, we have $A > B$, $A > C$, $B > D$, $C > D$, and $A > D$. B and C are not comparable, because B has a 0 where C has a 1 and C has a 0 where B has a 1. Comparability can be enforced by using weighted sums or other composition rules that specify how the various facets are used in an integrating function. In FT, composition rules are avoided, because such functions are rarely theoretically justifiable.

In that existence of a partial order for structuples with facets that have a common range is trivial, falsifiability has to be introduced from the outside. In FT, this typically means that one is looking for a correspondence between facets and regions in a representational space of the partially ordered structuples.

POSA and Conjoint Measurement

Content structuples typically are coupled with observations pertaining to them. In Chapter 1, duration judgments were observed under a variety of conditions defined by four-faceted structuples, establishing an observation function with four arguments. In such a case, a testable hypothesis is that the order of the observations corresponds to the order of the structuples, assuming a monotone relation of each design facet to the common observational range. That is, a "composition rule" or function f with n arguments for the structuples $(x_1, x_2, \ldots, x_n)$ is assumed which is monotone in each argument. This excludes disordinal interactions of the facets relative to the observations. Figure 1.1 illustrates a case in which such a partial order hypothesis is tested.

The hypothesis is closely related to conjoint measurement (CM). CM tests whether some monotonic transformation of the observations over the content structuples can be explained by a composition of appropriately transformed facets of Q. An example for such a hypothesis is that each observation $f(x_i, y_j)$ is monotonically related to $g(x_i) + h(y_j)$, in which g and h are arbitrary functions and x_i and y_j are elements of Facets X and Y, respectively. Hence, CM also attempts to explain the order of the observations from the facets and in the case of the usual additive model, without using "interaction" terms. CM is simultaneously more and less restrictive than a partial order hypothesis. It uses a more restrictive model—that is, a composition rule that does not exclude any pairs as incomparable—yet, it is also more general insofar as it does not restrict the functions g and h to be monotone.

Two-Dimensional Partially Ordered Structuple Sets

Basic Notions

One can go further and ask for the dimensions that span a partially ordered set. This means, in a sense, that we want to know what pulls the elements away from a linear order into different directions. An answer may be found with the help of POSAC (*Partial Order Scalogram Analysis with base Coordinates*; Shye, 1985a, 1994b).

Consider an example from Shye and Elizur (1976). They conducted a study based on the following categorical mapping sentence.

Individual (i) → is worried about losing his/her

$F1$		$F2$		$F3$		$F4$
interest		experience		stability		employment
(yes)	and	(yes)	and	(yes)	and	(yes)
(no)		(no)		(no)		(no)

following the introduction of a computer to his/her work unit

TABLE 10.3   Data Structuples of Concern About Loss of Interest, Expertise, Stability, and Employment Following the Introduction of Computers at the Workplace[a]

	interest	experience	stability	employment	freq
1	0	0	0	0	85
2	0	0	0	1	38
3	0	0	1	0	28
4	1	0	0	0	3
5	0	1	0	1	18
6	0	0	1	1	37
7	1	0	1	0	2
8	1	1	0	0	5
9	0	1	1	1	5
10	1	0	1	1	2
11	1	1	1	0	2
12	1	1	1	1	53

SOURCE: Shye and Elizur (1976).
NOTES: a. 1 = concerned, 0 = not concerned; freq = frequency of structuple.

Each individual was asked to indicate whether he or she was worried about the four possibilities of loss. If every structuple that is logically possible would have been empirically observed, there would have been $2^4 = 16$ possible data structuples. All of these possibilities did occur, but with different frequencies: 98% of the persons responded with one of the 12 structuples listed in Table 10.3 (observed scalogram).

These structuples can be ordered, in that a 1 (Yes) always means more in terms of worries than a 0 (No). However, the structuples do not form a one-dimensional scale. Yet it is always possible to partially order such structuples with a common order on their facets. Two Hasse diagrams are shown in Figure 10.6. Both are formally equivalent, but the one on the right-hand side looks simpler, because it does not have paths that cross each other. If this is so, one can represent the partially order set of structuples by two base coordinate scales.

Figure 10.7 shows a perfect POSAC solution—together with a system of partitioning lines—for the same data. The configuration is related to the right-hand graph in Figure 10.6 by a 45 degree rotation to the right and by some alignments of the point locations (to be explained later). It has the property that the points in the lower left-hand quadrant of each point are below (less than) this point in terms of the partial order; points in the upper right-hand quadrant are above (greater than) this point in the same sense; and points within the upper left-hand and lower right-hand quadrants are not comparable to the respective point of interest.

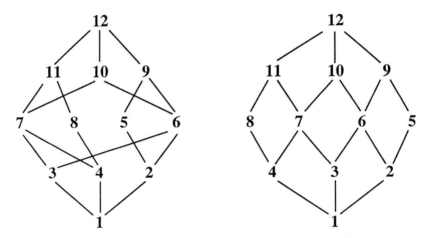

Figure 10.6. Two Partial Order Diagrams for the Structuples of Table 10.3

We now look at the configuration in terms of its a priori content, which generates the grid system in Figure 10.7. Concentrating on the first struct of the structuples (i.e., the first item) and ignoring all others leads to the item diagram in the upper left-hand panel of Figure 10.8. It shows, as indicated, that the first item with its F1 range induces a simple partitioning of the points: two regions emerge depending on the points' Y-coordinates only. A similar partitioning is induced by F4, but this time with respect to the X-coordinate only (lower right-hand panel of Figure 10.8). Thus, F1 and F4 endow the Y- and X-axes, respectively, with their primary meaning (*polar* range facets or polar items). Losing employment and losing interest are therefore the two "basic worries."

The roles of Facets F2 and F3 are secondary ones. They can be understood from the other two diagrams of Figure 10.8. F2 *accentuates* the possibilities to discriminate between points that are high X or Y or both. F2 splits the upper halves of X and Y, respectively, into two intervals. Persons who indicate that they are worried about losing stability (i.e., who have a 1 on F2) fall into the upper-most regions of X or of Y or of both, just as if being worried about losing stability accentuates the basic worries of interest or employment or both. The role of Facet F3, in contrast, is *attenuating* so that persons with high scores on F3 are relatively similar on their X and Y coordinates. F3, however, allows for finer distinctions on the lower end of the X and Y scales: Persons who indicate that they are *not* worried about losing stability must be *very* low on both basic worries, X

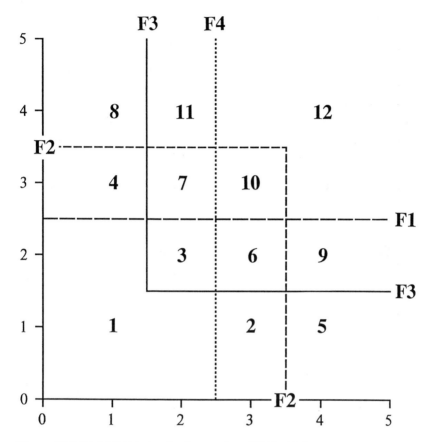

Figure 10.7. POSAC Solution for Structuples of Table 10.6

NOTE: Figure 10.7 shows the partition lines induced by Facets F1 = interest, F2 = experience, F3 = stability, F4 = employment, respectively.

or *Y*. Together, the accentuating and the attenuating items induce a finer division on the *X* and *Y* base coordinates, promoting the possibility for theory-based measurement scales.

Principles of POSAC/Lattice Space Analysis

POSAC solutions are conveniently found by the program POSAC/Lattice Space Analysis (LSA). Its mathematical foundations are described fully in Shye (1985a). In POSAC, order relations (comparability as well

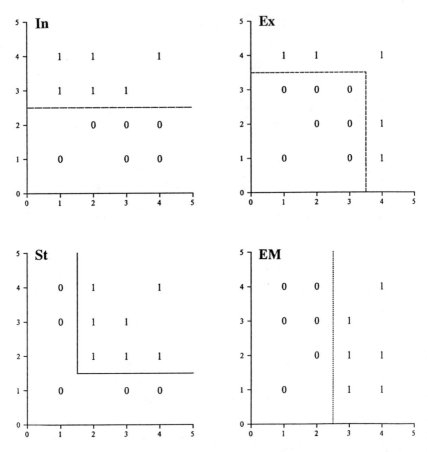

Figure 10.8. Facet Diagrams Over POSAC Solution of Figure 10.7 and Facets In, Ex, St, and Em, Respectively

as incomparability of the structuples) are considered as the essential empirical-substantive aspect of the data to be preserved in the data analysis. (This specification yields a generalized notion of "measurement" which is not confined to a single scale.) The purpose of POSAC, then, is to identify the smallest number, m, of scales—that is, new ordered ranges, $X_1, \ldots, X_m$—into which observed structuples (i.e., mostly persons) may be mapped one-to-one, so that the observed relations of order and incomparability are retained by the images in the mapping range $X = X_1 \times \ldots \times X_m$. That is,

(*) $a > b$ iff $(x_{a1}, \ldots, x_{am}) > (x_{b1}, \ldots, x_{bm})$,

(**) $a \blacklozenge b$ iff $(x_{a1}, \ldots, x_{am}) \blacklozenge (x_{b1}, \ldots, x_{bm})$,

in which a and b are structuples with n structs; $(x_{a1}, \ldots, x_{am})$ and $(x_{b1}, \ldots, x_{bm})$ are their respective coordinate vectors in X, sought by POSAC; $>$ is defined so that $v = (v_1, \ldots, v_n)$ is greater than $w = (w_1, \ldots, w_n)$ iff at least one element of v, v_i, is greater than the corresponding element of w, w_i, and no element of v is smaller than the corresponding element of w; and $\blacklozenge$ is incomparability, that is, not $v > w$, not $w > v$, and not $v = w$.

$X_1, X_2, \ldots, X_m$ are called the POSAC scales, and m is the partial-order dimensionality of the observed scalogram. A one-dimensional scalogram (i.e., a scalogram with $m = 1$) is called a Guttman scale.

Here is an example. The mapping of the observed Structuples 2, 4, and 9 of Table 10.3,

2:0001 → (3,1)

4:1000 → (1,3)

9:0111 → (4,2)

is a perfect POSAC representation, because the order between 0111 and 0001 is retained by their images, (4,2) > (3,1), and so is the incomparability between 0111 and 1000 by (4,2) and (1,3) because 4 > 1 and 2 < 3. (For a graphic representation of this mapping, see Figure 10.7.)

If a perfect POSAC representation in a space of dimensionality 2 does not exist for a given scalogram, the program POSAC/LSA finds an optimal solution in terms of the coefficient of correct representation (CORREP), which specifies the proportion of structuple pairs, weighted by their observed frequencies, whose comparability and incomparability relations, respectively, are correctly represented. CORREP has bounds of 0 and 1 (perfect solution) (Shye & Amar, 1985). POSAC/LSA contains LSA-1 and LSA-2, two programs designed to aid the user in the interpretation of the POSAC solution—that is, in linking formal properties of the solution to substantive notions of the design (see below).

POSAC scales are studied and interpreted by observing the relationships between the item contents and the roles they play in structuring the POSAC space: the regions they induce in that space and, in particular, the divisions they induce on the scales. The content of an item that is monotonically related to an axis imparts its meaning to that scale, as a first approximation. Other items may serve to refine successively that meaning so as to systematically formulate the scale's meaning, as we illustrated in the previous section. A statistical analysis of logical roles played by items in structuring the POSAC space is facilitated by Lattice Space Analysis (LSA) of the items (Shye, 1985a). As an illustration, consider the example of the previous section. Its LSA-2 diagram looks as follows:

F3
(stability)

F1   F4
(interest)   (employment)

F2
(experience)

LSA-2 represents each item as a point. The horizontal position of a point tells us to what extent the item is monotonically correlated with the X_1 axis more than with the X_2 axis of a two-dimensional POSAC representation of these items. On the extreme right and extreme left, then, we find the two polar items—the ones associated most with the X_1 axis and the one associated most with the X_2 axis, respectively. Here, we see that F4 and F1 are the two polar items imparting their meanings, as first approximations, to the X_1 and X_2 POSAC scales, respectively (see also Figures 10.7 and 10.8). The vertical position of a point, on the other hand, indicates whether the item in question plays the role of an attenuator (top) or of an accentuator (bottom). When the number of items is large, LSA provides a useful overview of the items' contributions to shaping the meanings of the POSAC scales.

A recent, more intricate example of POSAC/LSA is its application to the multiple scaling of public attitudes toward U.S. foreign policy (Russett & Shye, 1993).

LSA-1 is yet another procedure that maps the items of the two-dimensional POSAC by information drawn from POSAC's boundary ("enveloping") scales into a two-dimensional content space. A boundary scale is a scale ("chain") that starts with the maximal structuple (e.g., 111..1) and ends with the minimal stuctuple (000..0). It contains all structuples that are at the boundary of the POSAC diagram. It can be shown that, under certain conditions, these scales contain the essentials of the entire scalogram, so that the resultant map is simply an item similarity representation (see SSA later in this chapter) with respect to a particular coefficient of structural similarity, E^*, defined between items in a given item set. This procedure constitutes the link between the POSAC representation (which is based on the rows) and the SSA representation (which is based on the columns) of the scalogram (Theorems 9 and 10 in Shye, 1985a).

In spite of its algebraic complexity, E^* has a simple, intuitive meaning: Given a scalogram in n items, for any two items, u and v, E^*_{uv} assesses the extent to which the values of u and v mutually coincide (rather than differ) simultaneously with a *larger* (rather than smaller) variety of substructuples in the remaining n-2 items of the scalogram. Thus, E^* is pairwise, but, in the spirit of FT, is "context dependent" in that its value (ranging between -1 and $+1$) does depend on the set of content-representative items, processed together.

POSAC for Polychotomous Items

The previous example on worries (Figures 10.8-10.10) is particularly simple, because each facet has only two elements. A POSAC analysis is, however, not restricted to dichotomous data. Dancer (1990b), for example, collected responses on five items culled from the suicide probability scale (SPS) on the basis of a mapping sentence on *adjustment*. The SPS provides, according to Dancer (1990b),

> a self-report measure assessing several aspects of psychological adjustment thought to be useful for identifying suicide risk in adolescents and adults. The measure is composed of 36 Likert-type items, each having four response categories ranging from "none or a little of the time" to "most or all of the time." (p. 491)

The response categories were coded as 1, 2, 3 and 4 (4 = *most or all of the time*), respectively. A high score was conceived by Dancer (1990b) as an index of maladjustment, an interpretation that follows from looking at the question part of the items: (a) In order to punish others I think of suicide, (b) I feel people would be better off if I were dead, (c) I feel it would be less painful to die than to keep living the way things are, (d) I have thought of how to do myself in, and (e) I think of suicide. One hundred respondents generated 38 different data structuples, ranging from 11111 (best adjustment) to 44444 (worst adjustment). They are shown in Table 10.4. The column labeled as *sum of category ranks* in this table refers to the common range of the items: A high sum is an index of general maladjustment.

It is possible to represent the structuples in Table 10.4 quite well (CORREP = 0.93) in the POSAC diagram shown in Figure 10.9. The facet

TABLE 10.4 Data Structuples Observed for 100 Persons in Response to Five
SPS Items (A, . . . , E) Described in Text[a]

ID	A	B	C	D	E	sum	freq.
1	4	4	4	4	4	20	5
2	4	4	3	4	4	19	1
3	4	2	4	3	4	17	1
4	2	4	4	3	4	17	1
5	4	4	3	3	3	17	1
6	3	3	3	4	3	16	1
7	3	3	3	3	3	15	1
8	3	2	4	3	2	14	1
9	1	3	4	3	3	14	1
10	2	4	3	3	2	14	1
11	4	4	3	1	2	14	1
12	2	4	3	2	2	13	1
13	3	2	2	2	3	12	1
14	1	3	4	2	2	12	1
15	1	4	4	1	2	12	1
16	2	3	3	2	2	12	1
17	1	4	4	1	1	11	1
18	2	3	2	2	2	11	1
19	1	4	3	1	2	11	1
20	2	3	3	2	1	11	1
21	2	2	2	2	2	10	3
22	1	4	1	2	2	10	1
23	2	1	2	2	2	9	1
24	1	2	4	1	1	9	1
25	3	1	1	1	3	9	1
26	3	2	1	1	2	9	1
27	1	1	1	4	2	9	1
28	2	2	2	1	2	9	1
29	1	2	2	1	2	8	1
30	2	1	1	2	2	8	2
31	2	1	2	2	1	8	1
32	1	1	2	2	2	8	3
33	1	2	1	2	1	7	1
34	1	1	1	2	2	7	1
35	1	2	2	1	1	7	1
36	2	1	1	1	1	6	1
37	1	1	1	2	1	6	6
38	1	1	1	1	1	5	48

SOURCE: Dancer (1986).
NOTES: a. sum = sum of structuple elements; freq. = frequency of structuple in the sample.

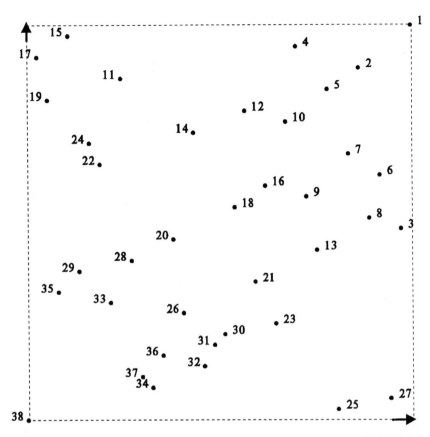

Figure 10.9. POSAC Diagram for Structuples for Adjustment Data From Table 10.4

diagram for Item D in Figure 10.10 shows that this item plays a polar role, inducing roughly parallel regions that are ordered in the sense of the common range (from low to high maladjustment). These regions are also ordered along the *X* axis. Item D, therefore, is found to have a particularly simple relation to the *X* axis: The more maladjusted a respondent is in the sense of Item D, the higher he or she lies on the *X* axis of the POSAC diagram. The *Y* axis shows an analogous relation to Item B (Figure 10.11). Item C—which correlates highly with Item B—behaves similarly. The other items play secondary roles. It is easy to check that Item A is an attenuator, whereas Item E induces a partition along the joint direction.

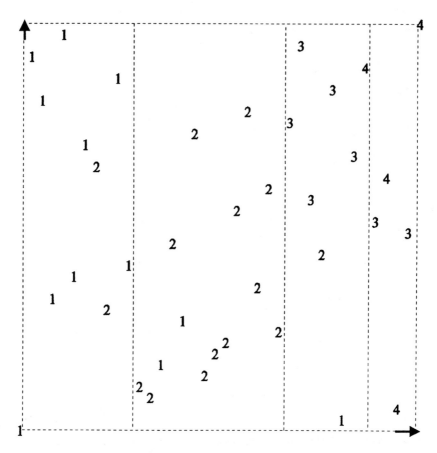

Figure 10.10. Facet Diagram for Facet D Acting on POSAC Diagram of Figure 10.9

What do these findings mean? Dancer (1990b) notes, in particular that

the key to understanding a partial order structure rests in relating the X- and the Y-base directions of the solution space to conceptual components of the base items. This analysis suggests that the affective expressions of psychological adjustment, restricted in this analysis to manifestations of coping behavior as measured by SPS items [B and C], and cognitive expressions, as assessed by item [D], represent basic elements that characterize the partial order structure. (p. 494)

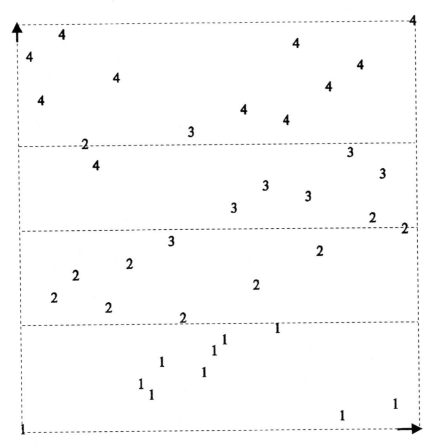

Figure 10.11. Facet Diagram for Facet B Acting on POSAC Diagram of Figure 10.9

Families of POSAC Configurations

Practical experience with POSAC and its application, as well as some of the mathematical results, have been limited so far to $m = 2$, which is the lowest dimensionality permitting the representation of incomparability relations between structuples. A useful approach to POSAC is to identify families of two-dimensional POSAC configurations and check empirical data against them as models. The advantage of these models is that a generic interpretation for their scales already exists. The simplest example of such a family is the diamond configuration, which for dichotomous data is characterized by the following condition: Given the scalogram, there exists a permutation of the items such that in each of the structuples there is at most one run (sequence) of high scores (Shye, 1985a; see also Coombs & Smith, 1973). Thus, 000111100 would be, but 001100011 would not be a diamond structuple (assuming the necessary permutation of the items has been performed). The LSA of the diamond configuration looks like an arc, and its generic interpretation is that of a simple rise and fall process. Other configurations, such as the "action system scalogram," have been studied as well (Shye, 1985a, 1985b).

External Variables in POSAC

As in MSA, one can label the points in a POSAC representation with values of an external variable in order to see if the distinctions that this variable makes among the observed structuples are mirrored in the distribution of the points in space. The POSAC/LSA program allows the user to combine several external variables into an "external trait," in effect a dichotomous variable specifying whether the defined trait (e.g., young educated female) does (1) or does not (0) characterize a subject. Then, for each structuple—which may of course be shared by any number of subjects—the program records the proportion of subjects with that given structuple that have a defined trait. The proportions are coded and plotted on the POSAC space to permit exploration for regions with high (or low) occurrences of the trait. Additionally, the program prints the monotone correlation between the trait (that is, the dichotomous variable) and each of the following POSAC axes X, Y, J ($X + Y$ or "joint direction") and L ($X - Y$ or "lateral direction").

Levy & Guttman (1985) report a POSAC analysis, in which structuples of symptoms of thyroid cancer are studied. A number of background variables was available on the patients, for example information on whether they died of a particular cancer. The POSAC space revealed that only patients whose score on the joint direction ($X + Y$) was above a certain value, died. Substantively expressed, this means that the lethal risk is reflected by the sum of the basic symptoms. A number of other background variables also showed simple relationships to the basic symptoms. They occurred, for example, only if the patient was above a certain threshold value on X or on Y, respectively.

Dancer (1990b), in the suicide study discussed previously, found that people who atttempted suicide occupied the upper-right hand corner of the POSAC diagram in Figure 10.9. They were clearly separated from other (no risk) respondents who had relatively low scores on the joint direction.

Shye and Savelzon (1993) report a "POSAC discriminant analysis" in which a system of eight scientific well-being items, observed on a large sample of Russian immigrant scientists, played the role of criteria (predictor) variables. The items assessed the extent to which scientists have: (a) freedom of scientific activity, (b) opportunity to exercise scientific talent, (c) good professional atmosphere at work, (d) access to scientific publications, (e) opportunities to meet scientists from different countries and to participate in conferences, (f) necessary assistance of technical personnel, (g) equipment required for research, and (h) funding needed for research. The scientists were also asked whether they had adapted professionally in Israel, and this question played the role of the dependent variable or external trait.

POSAC identified 31 different scientific well-being data structuples and mapped them into the two-dimensional POSAC space with a satisfactory CORREP of 0.93. The axes were interpreted to represent primarily scientific well-being in the sense of infrastructure (X axis) and scientific well-being in the sense of external interactions (Y axis). The outcome (predictand) variable was the overall professional adjustment of the immigrant scientists. The resulting partition lines in the POSAC representation of the well-being items satisfactorily separated between the scientists who had high, average, and low adjustment. Figure 10.12 shows the POSAC solution, in which the points are marked as H, A, or L, followed by a number or a star. The letters indicate high, average, or low frequencies of the respondents on the external trait. For example, an H indicates that a relatively high proportion of respondents with that particular profile said "Yes, I have adapted professionally in Israel." The numbers following the letters indicate the profile frequency and a star indicates a frequency of 10 or more.

The partition lines in Figure 10.12 provide the right classification for 81% of the respondents. The misclassified profiles are underlined. Moreover, if we make a distinction only between the profiles with an average or high proportion of the possession of the external trait versus profiles with low such proportions, the one (top right) partition line would provide a classification with a single error (the profile marked L2 near the top of the right corner).

Logically, POSAC discriminant analysis used as such is but a special case of applying the POSAC/LSA external-variables feature to a situation in which the external trait (see above) is a variable (a) sharing a common range with the (internal) items processed by POSAC and (b) whose content has the significance of summary on global character relative to the items processed by POSAC. Technically, POSAC discriminant analysis requires

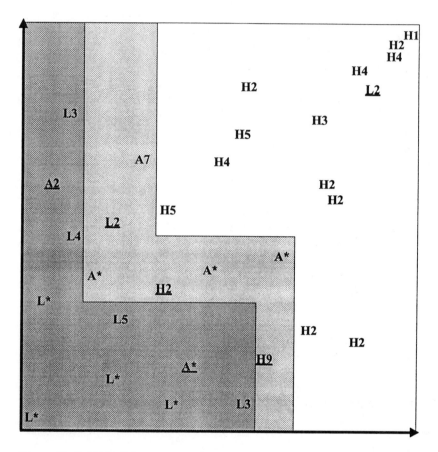

Figure 10.12. POSAC Space of Well-Being Items, With Points Replaced by Degree-of-Adjustment Index of Represented Persons

partitioning the POSAC space into two regions, by the best line that looks like a step function of Y on X, leaving as many as possible of the subjects with the defined trait on the upper-right region and as many as possible of the subjects without that trait on the lower left region.

Using Item Diagrams for Calibrating Coordinate Scales

POSAC scales, X, Y, (and in general X_a, $a = 1, \ldots, m$) embody parsimoniously the essential information regarding order relations (comparability and incomparability) among observed score structuples (profiles). It is important, therefore, to interpret them, in that the notions they assess are in a sense more fundamental than those of the items sampled for observation. Furthermore, once interpreted, it is useful to divide each of the m coordinate scales into ordered equivalence-intervals. These, in turn, will assign to each person m scores (one for each coordinate scale), giving rise to a "derived" structuple (profile) which is shorter than the original one $(2 < n;$ and in general, $m < n)$ and may tap the essential contents of the universe investigated.

While LSA1 and LSA2 can be useful in interpreting the POSAC axes, the item diagrams (each showing how an item partitions the POSAC space by the item values) are essential for calibrating the POSAC scales, X, Y—that is, for determining the (ordered) equivalence-intervals on each coordinate scale. The calibrating procedure is based simply on letting the x,y coordinates of the bending points (and of the end points) of each partition line in each item diagram determine equivalence-interval boundary points on the X, Y coordinate scale.

In searching for partition lines in an item diagram, one looks for those that appear to be eligible only: that is, those that resemble a monotone step function (see Lemma 7 in Shye, 1985a). Moreover, in that not every set of eligible partition lines is an eligible set (see Theorem 11 in Shye, 1985a), one should take care that in the set finally adopted, lines conform to the logic of POSAC. The identification of such lines is supported by the computer program POSACSEP (Shye, in press). POSACSEP's algorithm is outlined in the following.

On the Algorithm for Partitioning the POSAC Space

We are given a set of objects (i.e., score structuples) partitioned into two subsets, 0 and 1, and a mapping of the objects into the two-dimensional POSAC "square" 100×100, so that each object i has coordinates (x_i, y_i) with $0 \leq x_i \leq 100$ and $0 \leq y_i \leq 100$. We want to partition the square into two regions by a line so that, as well as possible, points pertaining to subset 0 are in one region and points pertaining to subset 1 are in the other region, subject to the following condition. The partition line separating the two regions is a continuous line consisting of horizontal and vertical sections. The line starts at an initial point on the upper edge $(y = 100)$ or left edge $(x = 0)$ of the square and descends monotonically to the lower edge $(y = 0)$ or right edge $(x = 100)$ of the square, by sections with nondecreasing values of x and nonincreasing values of y (Shye, 1985a).

The partition line separates the region 1, always taken as containing the upper right-hand corner (100, 100), from the region 0, always containing the lower-left hand corner (0, 0). The problem now is the following: given two sets of points (x,y) each assigned to subset 0 or 1, generate the "best" partition line of this type with a given number of corners. The best line is defined as that which minimizes the sum of the deviations of points from their correct region. Deviations are measured for each proposed line by identifying the points that fall on the wrong side of the line, measuring the deviation of each such point from its region (defined as the least city-block distance, that is, the distance measured along X and Y, respectively, from the point to the line) and summing the deviations over the points. In the case in which such points represent profiles with a frequency greater than 1, the contribution to the deviation is weighted by the frequency of the profile. (It should be noted that, for the purpose of computing the deviations, the edges of the square are not regarded as part of the partition line.)

To solve the problem, a minimum search routine has been developed using the downhill simplex method (Nelder & Mead, 1965; Press, Flannery, Teukolsky, & Vetterling, 1986).[3] The routine was implemented by labeling a given partition line by the x and y values of the various sections, so that a line of five corners and six sections can be described by six numbers. Various values of these numbers that might arise in the course of the minimization describe an illegal boundary—one which extends beyond the 100×100 square or is not monotonic. Such cases are handled by heavily penalizing the loss function. This results in the simplex in the minimization routine bouncing off the walls of the infinite potential well thus created.

The initial approximation to a partition line is taken as a roughly central "staircase," with the separate linearly independent points of the simplex generated by successively almost closing up the largest gap. In situations in which the method is used with successive increases in the number of corners, it is possible to set an initial approximation by adding a section to the optimum found with one less section. This guarantees successive improvement of the solution, but carries the danger of getting stuck in a local minimum, which becomes nonoptimal for a higher number of corners. For the moment, it has been decided to restart the search in the center for every case. If it is found that nonoptimal solutions are generated—for example, the solution with five corners being less good than that with four—it is possible to add a separate search based on the previous experience and to use the better of the two results thus generated. The POSAC-SEP subroutine produces optionally, for each POSAC item and for partition-line types with 0, 1, 2, 3 corners a screen map showing the

TABLE 10.5 POSACSEP Results for the POSAC Diagram in Figure 10.7

Item	Polar		ACC/ATT		Promoting		Modifying	
1	.00	Y	.00	C	.00	Y	.00	C
2	72.73	Y	.00	C	.00	Y	.00	C
3	72.73	Y	.00	T	.00	Y	.00	C
4	.00	X	.00	C	.00	Y	.00	C

solution reached in each case. In addition, the program produces a table showing, for each item and each line type, the total deviations. Table 10.5 is the POSACSEP result for the items (Range Facets F1, . . . , F4) of the Shye-Elizur study (Figure 10.7).

In accordance with POSAC item-role analysis (Shye 1985a), POSAC-SEP evaluates each item with respect to each of four possible roles, as follows:

- *Polar* role characterizes an item whose partition line has no corners. The two possible shapes are called X-polar (i.e., with the partition line parallel to the Y-axis), and Y-polar (with the partition line parallel, the X-axis). The program selects and presents in the table the better one only, and records (by X or Y) which one it is.

- *ACC/ATT* role (accentuating or attenuating role) characterizes an item whose partition line has one corner. The two possible shapes are an inverted-L-shaped partition line (normally representing an accentuating item) and an L-shaped partition line (normally representing an attenuating item). The program selects and presents in the table the better one, only, and records (by a C or T, respectively) which one it is.

- *Promoting* role characterizes an item whose partition line has two corners. The program selects and presents in the table the better one of the two possible shapes and records (by X or Y) which one it is, thus: if the partition line starts and ends by bisecting the lines $y = 100$ and $y = 0$, respectively, it is marked X (for X-promoter). If the partition line starts and ends by bisecting the lines $x = 0$ and $x = 100$, respectively, it is marked Y (for Y-promoter).

- *Modifying* role characterizes an item whose partition line has three corners. The program selects and presents in the table the better one of the two possible shapes and records (by C or T) which one it is. If the partition line modifies a partition line of an accentuating item it is marked C. If the partition line modifies a partition line of an attenuating item it is marked T.

Inspecting Table 10.5, we find that for Item 1 a Y-polar partition has been found, with no (.00) deviation. Hence Item 1 plays a Y-polar role. For Item

2 the program found that its fit to a polar role is poor (deviation of 72.73 units), but its fit to an accentuating role (marked by 'C') is perfect. Similarly we find that Item 3 is attenuating and Item 4 is the other polar—X-polar—item, as discussed above.

In more complex empirical data, studying POSACSEP table can help determine the optimal role assignments for the processed items. The result is a model that enables a rationalized measurement of the contents observed.

Notes

1. Consider an analogy. Take the number 1.414. It is a good solution to the problem "find the square root of 2." This is easy to check by multiplying 1.414 by itself. One does not have to know how the solution 1.414 was found.

2. In principle, POSAC can be applied to data structuples with a common range and also to content structuples whose facets are all ordered in the same sense (as, e.g., in the Bastide & van den Berghe, 1957, example discussed in Section 4.3.2). In practice, however, POSAC is almost always used on data structuples, whose facets are the range facets and whose elements are typically observed scores.

3. In this section the term *simplex* means "the geometrical figure consisting, in N dimensions, of N + 1 points (or vertices) and all their interconnecting line segments, polygonal faces, etc. In two dimensions, a simplex is a triangle. In three dimensions, it is the tetrahedron, not necessarily the regular tetrahedron. The simplex method of linear programming also makes use of the geometrical concept of a simplex" (Press et al., 1986, p. 290).

The minimum search routine has the advantage that, although it is quite inefficient in terms of the number of function evaluations required, it lays no particular geometrical requirements on the function being minimized. It only tests the actual values of the function to determine which of several values is the minimum and does not use derivatives or assign any significance to differences of values.

The algorithm was developed with Dr. Roger Kingsley.

Hypotheses for Similarity Structures

- Some Notes on SSA
- Regional Hypotheses: An Overview
- Basics of Testing Regional Hypotheses
- General Considerations on Partitions
- Regional Hypotheses in Ongoing Research
- Regions and Dimension Systems
- Regional Hypotheses and Other Statistical Approaches

Similarity data come in different forms. The typical case is a correlation matrix for a battery of items, that is, a particular form of structuple similarity (the subject covered in Chapter 10). Another variant is a distance matrix that contains coefficients measuring the dissimilarity of data structuples (usually over persons). Similarities can also be collected directly. In psychophysics, for example, it is common practice to directly rate the (dis)similarity of pairs of objects on numerical scales (e.g., from 0 = *same, identical* to 9 = *extremely dissimilar*).

In that the form of data analysis is part of the hypothesis, the choice of the similarity coefficient is of central importance (Guttman, 1982e). The common practice of mechanically using a convenient statistical coefficient such as the Pearson correlation coefficient is often difficult to rationalize. Moreover, employing a monotone correlation (Guttman, 1985a), a particular distance function or an S_i similarity measure (Gower, 1985), for example, may have a significant impact on the resulting similarity structure. Shye (1985a) proposed the coefficient of structural similarity, E*, as a "natural" similarity coefficient in that it enables a link between the dimensionalities of POSA and of SSA (see Chapter 10).

Similarity data, in any case, can be looked at in many ways. What has been found to be particularly revealing is to first represent them geometrically via distances in a multidimensional configuration of points. The dimensionality of the space is chosen to be as small as possible—smallest space analysis (SSA). Given such an "SSA" space, one then attempts to identify a correspondence between the definitional system and the SSA space: That is, one tries to partition the space, facet by facet, so that points that represent items with the same struct on a facet fall into the same region of the partition (*regional hypothesis*). The hypothesis, then, is that such a partitioning of the SSA space is possible. A further constraint is that the resulting regions must be *simple*. A special case of this hypothesis is studied in discriminant analysis.

Some Notes on SSA

SSA is an acronym for (multidimensional) *s*imilarity *s*tructure *a*nalysis. It was originally called *s*mallest *s*pace *a*nalysis (Guttman, 1968), and is widely known as MDS or *m*ulti*d*imensional *s*caling (Kruskal, 1964; Takane, Young & De Leeuw, 1977; Torgerson, 1958). Our use of the term *SSA* was suggested by Guttman (1991; see also Borg & Lingoes, 1987) to better characterize the nature and purpose of the technique, which is, first of all, to yield a geometric space of points whose distances represent similarity coefficients among a set of objects. To achieve such a representation in a space of small dimensionality is usually desirable (for reasons of economy, for example; the term *small* is taken from mathematics where it refers to algebraically minimal dimensionality). However, choosing a small dimensionality is neither always optimal for interpretation nor for recovering "true" distances in noisy data (overcompression, Sherman, 1972). On the other hand, the common practice to interpret MDS solutions by looking at the points' coordinate values (similar to interpreting factor analytic solutions), is most often unfounded on theoretical grounds. The term *MDS*, therefore, is somewhat misleading for the applied researcher, in that it suggests that "dimensions" must be meaningful.

Technically, then, SSA can be characterized as follows. Given a set of similarity coefficients, s_{ij}, for a set of objects, $i,j = 1, \ldots, n,$ a mapping into a point space of dimensionality m is sought such that

$$s_{ij} = f[d_{ij}(\mathbf{X})], \qquad \text{for all observed } s_{ij}, \qquad [1]$$

in which $d_{ij}(\mathbf{X})$ is a distance—the euclidean distance, in almost all applications—of the points i and j of configuration $\mathbf{X}$; f is the model function, typically a weakly descending monotone function or a linear function. If Equation 1 does not hold, an optimal solution is sought that minimizes some loss function. The loss function employed most often is *Stress* (Kruskal, 1964) and is defined as

$$\text{Stress} = \sqrt{\frac{\sum_{i<j} [f(s_{ij}) - d_{ij}(\mathbf{X})]^2}{\sum_{i<j} d_{ij}^2}} , \qquad [2]$$

or, for ordinal SSA only, the *coefficient of alienation* (Guttman, 1968), defined as

$$K = \sqrt{1 - \mu^2} , \text{ with } \mu = \frac{\sum d_{ij}(\mathbf{X})d_{ij}^*(\mathbf{X})}{\sqrt{\sum d_{ij}^2(\mathbf{X})\sum [d_{ij}^*(\mathbf{X})]^2}} , \qquad [3]$$

in which the variable $d_{ij}^*(\mathbf{X})$ is the "rank image" of $d_{ij}(\mathbf{X})$; that is, the $d_{ij}(\mathbf{X})$s are permuted so that their rank order corresponds to the rank order of the similarities s_{ij}.

Solving the SSA problem, thus, involves finding a point configuration $\mathbf{X}$ (with fixed dimensionality m) that defines the distances d_{ij}, and finding a regression function f of the distances onto the similarity data so that Stress = min or K = min. This proves to be a difficult optimization problem, but there exist refined algorithms that almost certainly find the best solution $\mathbf{X}$ (De Leeuw & Heiser, 1977, 1980; Groenen, 1994).

Various side constraints can be imposed onto the distances d_{ij} (Borg & Lingoes, 1980), the coordinates $\mathbf{X}$ (Bentler & Weeks, 1978), the matrix of similarity coefficients (conditionalities, weightings; see Takane et al., 1977), but they remain of little interest for most applications.[1]

The typical SSA application proceeds as follows. Given a matrix of similarity or dissimilarity coefficients, an ordinal (f = monotone) SSA solution is sought in a number of dimensionalities, mostly starting with m = 2. Only if the plot of s_{ij} versus d_{ij} values (Shepard diagram) shows marked degeneracies (i.e., definite discontinuities of the regression trend, such as a simple step function) whereas, at the same time, the loss function converges toward zero, would one try a linear f, which is robust against such degeneracies. One then picks a solution with "acceptable" goodness of fit (stress, alienation) for interpretation. Acceptability depends on many considerations, such as the accuracy of the data representation relative to the reliability of the similarity coefficients, the number of points relative to the dimensionality of **X,** the robustness of the point configuration over replications, the interpretability of the point space, and the stability of this interpretation over replications, among other things. These criteria, obviously, cut so much into content matters that it is impossible to evaluate the issue of proper dimensionality in purely mathematical terms, but some guidance is provided by the results of extensive simulation studies (see Borg & Lingoes, 1987, Chapter 8).

Regional Hypotheses: An Overview

Regional hypotheses are by far the most successful kind of hypotheses developed in the FT context. A region (in a plane) is defined as a connected set of points such as the inside of a rectangle or a circle. A set is connected if each pair of its points can be joined by a curve all of whose points are in the set. A region is called simply connected if it has no holes—that is, if any closed curve within the region can be continuously contracted to each of the region's points without leaving the region.

Regional hypotheses link content facets to regions of the empirical SSA space. The hypothesis is that the SSA space can be partitioned such that each region represents a different facet element. That is, all points within a particular region should be associated with the same facet element and points in different regions should be associated with different facet elements. Regional hypotheses, therefore, are analogous to what is studied in discriminant analysis, in which one also asks if and how a set of points that represent elements of different classes (typically, groups of persons such as males and females) can be separated optimally into nonoverlapping sets. Discriminant analysis, however, only considers partition lines that are straight and parallel to each other. Regional hypotheses include this possibility as a special case.

The content facets often play one of three prototypical roles in this context: They partition the space in an *axial, radial* (modular), or *angular* (polar) way. An axial facet is one that corresponds to a linear pattern—the partitioning lines cut the space in a parallel fashion into simply ordered "stripes" (an axial *simplex* of regions; see Figure 1.4). A radial facet leads to a pattern that resembles a set of concentric bands (a radial simplex of regions; see Figure 1.5). Finally, an angular facet cuts the space, by rays emanating from a common origin, into sectors, similar to cutting a pie into pieces (*circumplex* of regions; see Figures 11.10 and 11.11).

A number of particular combinations of facets that play such roles lead to structures that were given special names because they are encountered frequently in practice. For example, the combination of an angular facet and a radial facet in a plane, having a common center, constitutes a *radex,* a structure similar to a dart board. Adding an axial facet in the third dimension renders a *cylindrex* (see Figure 11.4). Another interesting structure is a *multiplex,* a conjunction of at least two axial partitions (see Figures 11.6 through 11.8). Special cases of the multiplex are called *duplex* (two axial facets; see Figures 11.6 and 11.7), *triplex* (three axial facets; see Figure 11.8), and so forth. The multiplex corresponds to the usual (Cartesian) coordinate system ("dimensions") as a special case if the facets are (densely) ordered and the partition lines are straight, parallel, and orthogonal to each other.

There is also a variety of structures that are found less frequently in practice—for example, the *spherex* (polar facets in three-dimensional space) or the *conex* (similar to the cylindrex, but with radexes that shrink as one moves along the axial facet). We will come back to some of them below (see also Shye, 1978b, 1994e).

Basics of Testing Regional Hypotheses

Scale Level of Facets and Regions

To predict regional patterns requires one to first clarify the expected roles of the facets in the definitional framework. This involves, first of all, classifying the "scale level" of each facet. For ordered facets, one predicts a regional structure whose regions are also (linearly) ordered, so that the statement that some region R comes "before" another region R' has meaning. Geometrically, this relation can express itself in parallel regions as in Figure 1.4 or in concentric regions as in Figure 1.5. The order of the regions should mirror the order specified for the elements of the corresponding facet. For another facet, one may have a substantive reason to believe that its elements are circularly ordered. In such instances, an angular facet may be hypothesized. For qualitative facets, some simple partitionability of the point configuration into regions, each of whose points share the same facet element, is already interesting.

If one combines an angular and an axial facet and if the similarity data can be represented in a plane, one often obtains a radex. More generally, however, when no dependence is expected between the facets, the product of an angular and an axial facet results in a cylindrical surface (Shye, 1978d).

Distinguishing facets as qualitative and ordinal does not, however, ask for
what may be called the "true" scale level. Rather, it represents a "role
assignment" (Velleman & Wilkinson, 1993, p. 8) that reflects "hypotheses on
some features of certain experimental [i.e., empirical; IB&SS] regression
curves" (Guttman, 1977, p. 105). Hence, if one cannot develop a hypothesis
on the correspondence between some order of the facet's elements and an
order among observable regions, then the facet *is* qualitative. Such hypotheses
cannot, of course, be developed in a vacuum. They, therefore, remain context
related. To see this, consider the facet *color* = {red, yellow, green, blue,
purple}. One would be tempted to say, at first, that this is a nominal facet. Yet
with respect to similarity judgments on colors, color has been shown to be
ordered empirically, in a circular way (Indow, 1974). Furthermore, with
respect to the physical wave length of colors, color is linearly ordered. This
shows that here, too, the observational context cannot be ignored.

From Regions Back to the Data

Facet-induced regions are but geometrical representations of certain
patterns in the data. A facet that is mapped into a radial partitioning of a
two-dimensional SSA representation of a correlation matrix, for example,
implies that the average correlation of the items tends to be greater for
points located in central regions of the system of concentric (hyper-)bands.
Similarly, an axial facet allows one to permute the correlation matrix into
a pattern of ordered blocks of items, in which the correlations between
items of different blocks tend to become statistically smaller the farther
apart their facet elements. An algebraic characterization of such patterns,
however, is much more difficult and less practical than a description in
terms of their geometric representations (Lingoes & Borg, 1979).

How to Look at Higher-Dimensional Spaces

Complex data typically require higher-dimensional spaces for their
representation. This makes regional interpretations more difficult. One
usually looks at orthogonal projection planes of such spaces, as we did in
Figures 1.2 through 1.6. It has been found useful to choose those planes
that are spanned by principal components. The reasons why such planes
often "work" is not entirely known. Guttman (personal communication)
suggested that researchers may implicitly design their observations with
such structures in mind, but this is an open question.

Orthogonal planes are chosen over other planes, because finding structural correspondences in one plane are independent of what is going on in

the complement of the space: The structure, in a sense, "cuts through" the remaining space, just as a radex cuts through the space along the axial facet in a cylindrex. Yet for the discovery of higher-dimensional regions, it may not be sufficient to only study planar projections.

The question arises, then, of what should be done if one does not succeed in establishing a correspondence between the definitional system and regions in a high-dimensional space. The problem is that the correspondence may actually exist, but could not be identified through those perspectives that were used to look at the space. Procrustean methods to rotate the space to a particular target are of limited use in this context because of the generality of the regional hypotheses that usually cannot be properly expressed in terms of point parameters. The exact location of the various points is really irrelevant as long as they are in the "right" regions.

It is always possible, however, to analyze subsets of the items that have the same structs on facets that are not at the focus of interest at the time. If one analyzes these items separately, then, because one has controlled for one or several variance sources, a space of much lower dimensionality might suffice to represent their empirical structure. Consider the cylindrex in Figure 11.4, for example. If the point distribution was such that the cylindrex was obliquely located relative to the principal axes of the SSA space, it might be difficult to see. However, one could take all the items in which the communication is oral, manual, or by paper and pencil, respectively, and analyze them separately. This would reveal a radex in each case and, taken together, a cylindrex.

General Considerations on Partitions

Generalizing Beyond the Sample

Partitions of geometric configurations with few points are relatively easy to find. Because there is so much empty space, the exact shape of the partition lines is also quite indeterminate. More determinacy and greater falsifiability is brought about by increasing the number of items. Yet how should one proceed if one cannot add more points?

Consider an example. Table 11.1 shows a matrix of correlations among eight intelligence tests (Guttman, 1965a; Borg, 1994). The tests are classified by two facets, *content* = {N = numerical, G = geometrical} and *task* = {A = achievement, I = inference}. An inspection of the correlations reveals a gradient: The coefficients are highest along the main diagonal, then taper off as one moves away from the main diagonal, and rise again

TABLE 11.1 Intercorrelations of Eight Intelligence Tests, Together With Content Structuples[a]

Structuple		1	2	3	4	5	6	7	8
NA	1	1.00	.67	.40	.19	.12	.25	.26	.39
NA	2	.67	1.00	.50	.26	.20	.28	.26	.38
NI	3	.40	.50	1.00	.52	.39	.31	.18	.24
GI	4	.19	.26	.52	1.00	.55	.49	.25	.22
GI	5	.12	.20	.39	.55	1.00	.46	.29	.14
GA	6	.25	.28	.31	.49	.46	1.00	.42	.38
GA	7	.26	.26	.18	.25	.29	.42	1.00	.40
GA	8	.39	.38	.24	.22	.14	.38	.40	1.00

SOURCE: Guttman (1965a).
NOTES: a. N = numerical, G = geometrical, A = application and I = inference.

as one approaches the corners. This seems to support the contiguity principle, because the structuples form a circular pattern in terms of their similarity as measured by counting the number of common elements.

An SSA representation of this matrix, accordingly, shows an approximate circumplex of points (Figure 11.1). It is also possible, however, to partition this configuration by each facet in turn. In that the facets are only dichotomous and there are so few points, many possibilities exist. A duplex partition is shown in Figure 11.2. Another possibility is exhibited in Figure 11.3. Its somewhat peculiar appearance is motivated by thinking beyond the given sample of items—that is, by considering the *universe* of all intelligence tests. Figure 11.4 shows what has been found to hold for the universe (Guttman, 1970; Guttman & Levy, 1991). This universe structure (cylindrex) reflects three facets: the angular facet *content* = {verbal, numerical, geometrical}, the radial facet *performance* = {inference, application, learning}, and the axial facet *communication* = {oral, manual manipulation, paper, & pencil}. Even though the items in Table 11.1 are not differentiated with respect to communication and they only reflect four out of six possible distinctions on the first two facets, their SSA representation nevertheless reflects a section of this universe structure.

Thinking beyond what is observed is always desirable. Although, of course, it is impossible to say in general how this can be done. In any case, most researchers are typically interested in generalizing their findings, most often to the entire content universe, to additional populations, and over replications. The system of partition lines should therefore be robust in this respect and not attend too much to the particular sample. Simple partitions with relatively smooth cutting lines are typically better in this respect.

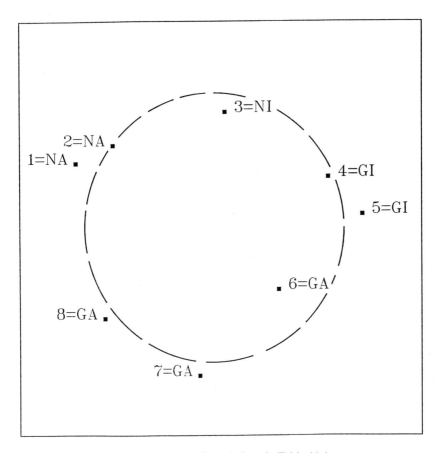

Figure 11.1. SSA Representation of Correlations in Table 11.1

NOTE: Broken lines indicate the approximately circular order of test items. For the meaning of structuples, see Table 11.1.

Errors and Simplicity of Regional Hypotheses

In Figures 1.1 through 1.4 and 11.2 through 11.4, partition lines were chosen that were as simple as possible. Simple partitions are, for example, those that consist not only of simply connected regions as in an axial or an angular system, but also the concentric bands of a circumplex. Therefore, *simple* means, above all, that the partition is simple to characterize in terms of the roles of the facets that induce the regions. Of course, if one were less restrictive with these figures and admitted greater irregularities (i.e., not requiring the lines to be so stiff locally), then the number of errors of classification could

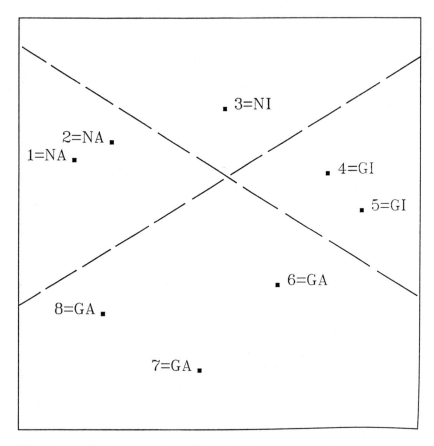

Figure 11.2. SSA Representation of Data in Table 11.1
NOTE: Lines partition space into *G*- vs. *N*-items, and into *A*- vs. *N*-items, respectively.

be reduced or even eliminated. Such error reduction has its price, however, because it makes it more difficult to describe the structure as such and, as a consequence, makes it harder to express how the facets "act" on the SSA space. Moreover, irregular ad-hoc partitions also reduce the likelihood in finding similar structures in replications and in the universe of items.

One thus faces a trade-off decision of the following kind. Should one use relatively simple partitions, even at the expense of a few errors? Or should one rather choose somewhat more irregular lines to avoid classification errors, and then leave it to the reader to simplify these patterns him- or herself? Obviously, there is no simple answer to this trade-off problem,

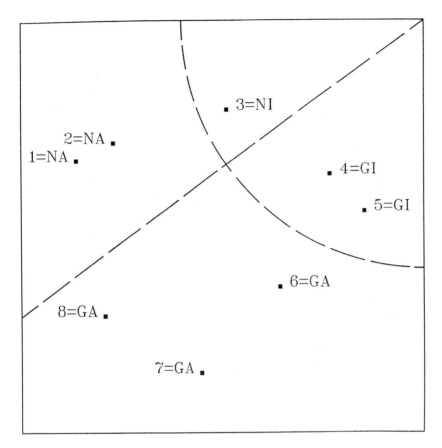

Figure 11.3. Alternative Partitioning of SSA Configuration of Test Items, With Curved Line Separating *A*- and *I*-Items

and one has to decide what seems most appropriate in the given context. Irregular lines, in any case, lead to the impression that partitioning a point configuration is not far from Rorschach diagnostics and casts doubts on the falsifiability of regional hypotheses.

Falsifiability of Regional Hypotheses

Generally, for the falsifiability of regional hypotheses, it is true what was demonstrated by the ping-pong balls thought experiment discussed previously in the MSA context. Regional patterns become quite unlikely

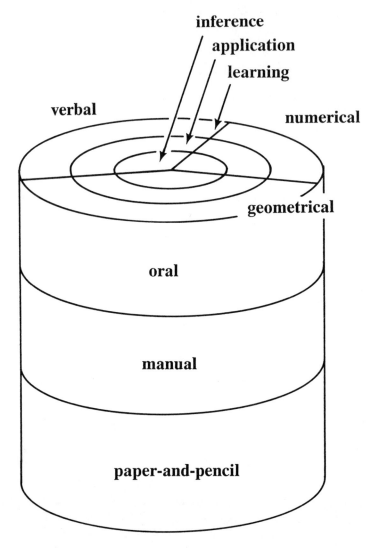

Figure 11.4. Structure of Universe of Intelligence Items (after Guttman & Levy, 1991), With Three Partitioning Facets

to result from chance the more points they succeed in classifying correctly, the more differentiated the system of facets is, the simpler the partition lines are and the greater the stability of the pattern over replications is.

For arbitrary structuples, one should not expect to find regional correspondences in the data. To see this, the following simulates this case by mixing the structuples in Table 11.1, so that they get randomly assigned to the items. Assume that this has led to the assignments 1 = GA, 2 = NI, 3 = GA, 4 = NA, 5 = GI, 6 = NA, 7 = GI, and 8 = GA. If we label the points in Figure 11.1 with these structuples, we find that the plane can be partitioned in a modular way by the facet {A,I}, but that the A-points are now in the center in between the I-points. This does not correspond to the structure of the content universe in Figure 11.4, which was replicated in hundreds of data sets.

The second facet, {G,N}, leads to a partitioning line that winds itself snakelike through the circular SSA configuration. It shows, in essence, that separating the G- from the N-points with a reasonably regular line is, in this given case, only possible because we have only eight points. It can hardly be expected, though, that such an artificial partition can be replicated in other data sets.

In addition to these rather formal criteria, one must request that the pattern of regions ultimately also makes sense. Yet irregular lines are already difficult to describe as such and, as a consequence, complicate the search for explaining the way in which the regions are related to the facets. Moreover, in the given case, the radial order of inference, application, and learning is not only replicable, but also seems to point to an ordered facet complexity, in which inference is the most complex task (see below). If application items, then, come to lie in the radex center, such further search for substantive meaning is thwarted.

Computerized Procedures for Testing Regional Hypotheses: Faceted SSA

To avoid seemingly arbitrary partitions, many users of regional hypotheses have asked for a more objective method for partitioning a space. Shye (1991b), in response to such requests, developed such a procedure. It partitions a facet diagram optimally in three ways: (a) in an axial way, by parallel and straight lines; (b) in a radial way, by concentric circles; and (c) in an angular way, by rays emanating from a common origin. These partition patterns enable convenient testing of the axial, radial, and angular regional hypotheses, respectively.

Consider an example. Figure 11.5 (top panel) shows a two-dimensional SSA representation of the intercorrelations of 13 items that asked for the importance of 13 work values. (These items will be examined more carefully later in this chapter.) The work values can be classified by various criteria (Table 11.2). Figure 11.5 (lower panel) shows the facet diagram

TABLE 11.2 Work Values, With Alternative Facetizations by Some Angular and Radial Facets[a]

No.	angular					radial		work value
	H	M	A	E	R	L	B	
1	m	a	g	k	i	g	3	interesting work
2	m	a	g	k	i	g	3	independence in work
3	m	a	g	k	i	g	3	work that requires much responsibility
4	m	a	g	k	i	n	4	job that is meaningful and sensible
5	m	r	g	k	e	i	1	good chances for advancement
6	m	r	r	a	s	i	1	job that is recognized and respected
7	h	b	r	a	s	n	4	job where one can help others
8	h	b	r	a	s	n	4	job useful for society
9	h	b	r	a	s	n	4	job with much contact to other people
10	.	s	r	.	.	.	.	(no item of this type given)
11	h	s	e	i	e	i	2	secure position
12	h	s	e	i	e	i	1	high income
13	h	p	e	i	e	n	4	job that leaves much spare time
14	h	p	e	i	e	n	4	safe and healthy working conditions

NOTES: a. H = *Herzberg* = {h = hygiene, m = motivators}; M = *Maslow* = {p = physiological, s = security, b = belongingness, r = recognition, a = self-actualization}; A = *Alderfer* = {e = existence, r = relations, g = growth}; E = *Elizur* = {i = instrumental-material, k = cognitive, a = affective-social}; R = *Rosenberg* = {e = extrinsic, i = intrinsic, s = social}; L = *Levy-Guttman* = {i = independent of individual performance, g = depends on group performance, n = not performance dependent}; B = *Borg-Elizur* = {1 = depends much on individual performance, 2 = depends more on individual performance than on system, 3 = depends both on individual performance and on system, 4 = depends on system only}.

for the classification into *instrumental* (1), *cognitive* (2), and *affective* (3) types. Both diagrams are screen dumps of an SSA solution produced by the Faceted SSA computer program, FSSA (Shye, 1991b).

Figure 11.6 shows three partitionings of the facet diagram. Starting on top, first note an axial partition, then a radial one, and finally an angular one. The goodness of the partition is measured by the facet separation index. (The computation of the facet separation index is described later in this chapter.) This index is based on the sum of distances—not just the number—of the "deviant" points from their respective regions. The facet separation index is equal to 1 if the partition is perfect; otherwise, it is less than 1. Hence, in the given example, although the separation indexes do not differ by much, the radial partition is best in terms of this index.

Taking into account wider criteria, the angular partition must be preferred, though. Separability in the radial case is slightly better, but Region 3 lies between 1 and 2. Hence, the regions are linearly ordered here, but the facet only makes nominal distinctions. Most importantly, the third partition pattern can be replicated (Elizur, Borg, Hunt, & Magyari-Beck, 1991; see also Figure

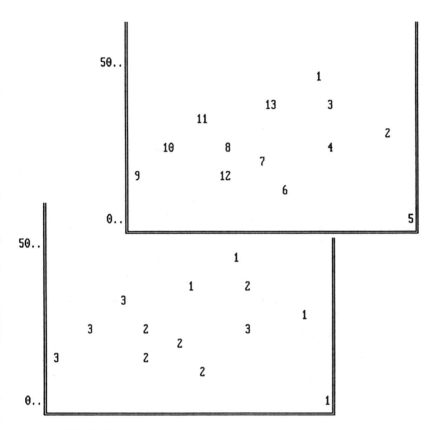

Figure 11.5. SSA Representation of Correlations of Work Value Items (upper panel) and a Facet Diagram for a Facet With Three Elements (lower panel)

NOTE: The representations are screen dumps of FSSA result.

11.9). Further considerations on choosing a particular partition will be discussed later in this chapter when this question is examined within an ongoing research perspective. None of these additional decision criteria can be integrated into a mechanical procedure that looks at only a given point space. Thus, as in SSA in general, computerized partitioning is valuable only to the extent to which the distribution of points in the SSA space is sufficiently dense and the points are representative for the respective facets to clearly distinguish between alternative partitionings. If this is not the case and the separation indexes are close to each other, additional considerations must be utilized to decide between competing partitions, as in the present example.

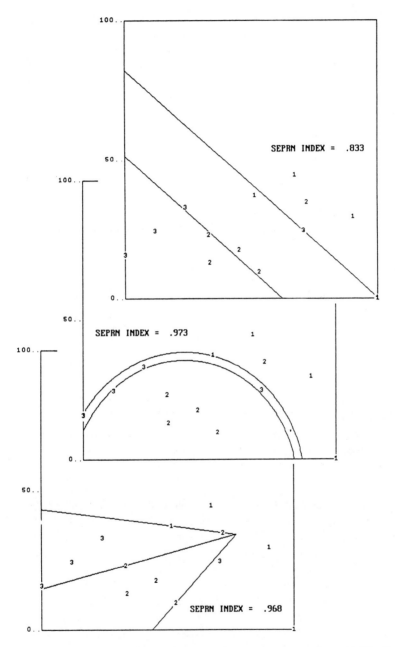

Figure 11.6. Computerized Partitions of Facet Diagram in Figure 11.5 by Parallel, Concentric, and Radial Lines, Respectively

Partitioning the SSA by Facets: Loss Functions and Separation Indexes

General Description

The Loss Function. The algorithm for optimally partitioning the two-dimensional SSA space into regions in accordance with an a priori facet (item classification) hinges on the loss function to be minimized. For each trial partition, some points may fall outside the region assigned to them by that partition. Such a point is called a *deviant* point. The loss function is made up of the sum of the distances of the deviant points from their assigned regions.

Normalization. Whereas the optimization algorithm works on the loss function only, a normalizing function is introduced to create a coefficient of goodness-of-fit for a computed space-partition. The normalizing function represents the typical value of the loss function for a set of points randomly and uniformly distributed in the 100×100 square into which item-points are plotted by the SSA. The resulting normalized loss function falls roughly on a scale between 0 and 1, in which 0 represents a perfect separation, with each item-point falling inside its assigned region.

The separation index is defined simply by subtracting the normalized loss function from 1, so that a separation index of 1 represents a perfect regional separation by the prespecified facet. The separation index is given by

$$\text{SEPRN INDEX} = 1 - \frac{loss\ function}{normalizing\ function} \qquad [4]$$

The Three Patterns. The algorithms in the Faceted SSA computer program permit testing for three different separation patterns, corresponding to the partitioning of the plane into regions (a) by straight parallel lines (axial facet), (b) by concentric circles (radial facet), or (c) by radii emanating from a central point (angular facet). For each pattern, an appropriate loss function has been defined and a normalization function has been computed.

Mathematical Formulation of the Separation Indexes

We are given a set A of n items, classified into k classes, $A_1, \ldots, A_k$, and a mapping of the items as points in the 100×100 square.

The Axial Case. We seek a set of $k - 1$ straight parallel lines whose partitioning of the plane corresponds to the given item classification. Let the j-th line, $x \times \sin \theta - y \times \cos \theta + c_j = 0$, be the one separating the region assigned to A_j from the region assigned to A_{j+1} ($j = 1, \ldots, k - 1$). The algebraic (signed) distance of an item-point (x_i, y_i) from the j-th line is given by $d_i^{AX}(j) = x_i \times \sin \theta - y_i \times \cos \theta + c_j$. The loss function for the axial case is therefore

$$L_{AXIAL}(\theta, c_1, \ldots, c_{k-1}) = \sum_{j = 1, \ldots, k-1} \left[\sum_{\substack{(x_i, y_i) \in A_j \\ d_i^{AX}(j) > 0}} d_i^{AX}(j) - \sum_{\substack{(x_i, y_i) \in A_{j+1} \\ d_i^{AX}(j) < 0}} d_i^{AX}(j) \right]. \qquad [5]$$

The normalizing term varies slightly with θ and reaches a minimum for $\theta = 45°$. Therefore, a conservative choice for the normalizing term would be the value of the loss function for that angle, which turns out to be

$$N_{AXIAL} = \frac{100\sqrt{2}}{6} \times \frac{n(k-1)}{k}. \qquad [6]$$

The separation index for the axial case, then, is

$$\text{AXIAL SEPRN INDEX} = 1 - \frac{L_{AXIAL}}{N_{AXIAL}}. \qquad [7]$$

The Radial Case. We seek a set of $k - 1$ concentric circles whose partitioning of the plane corresponds to the given item classification. Let the j-th circle $(x_i - X)^2 + (y_i - Y) = r_j^2$, with center at (X, Y) be the one separating the region assigned to A_j from the region assigned to A_{j+1} ($j = 1, \ldots, k - 1$). The algebraic (signed) distance of an item-point (x_i, y_i) from the j-th circle is given by

$$d_i^{RD}(j) = \sqrt{(x_i - X)^2 + (y_i - Y)^2} - r_j. \qquad [8]$$

The loss function for the radial case is, therefore,

$$L_{RADIAL}(X, Y, r_1, \ldots, r_{k-1}) = \sum_{j = 1, \ldots, k-1} \left[\sum_{\substack{(x_i, y_i) \in A_j \\ d_i^{RD}(j) > 0}} d_i^{RD}(j) - \sum_{\substack{(x_i, y_i) \in A_{j+1} \\ d_i^{RD}(j) < 0}} d_i^{RD}(j) \right] \qquad [9]$$

The normalizing term for the radial case has been computed to be

$$N_{RADIAL} = 100 \left[\frac{\sqrt{2} + \ln(1 + \sqrt{2})}{6} - \frac{1}{3}\sqrt{\frac{2}{\pi}} \right] \times \frac{n(k-1)}{k} . \qquad [10]$$

The separation index for the axial case, then, is

$$\text{RADIAL SEPRN INDEX} = 1 - \frac{L_{RADIAL}}{N_{RADIAL}} . \qquad [11]$$

The Angular Case. We seek a set of k radii emanating from a common center (X, Y) whose partition of the plane corresponds to the given item classification. Let the j-th radius, of angle θ_j, be the one separating the region assigned to A_j from the region assigned to A_{j+1} ($j = 1, \ldots, k$). The radius (half-line) may be defined as

$$\left\{ (x, y) \left| \begin{array}{c} x \times \sin\theta_j - y \times \cos\theta_j = X \times \sin\theta_j - Y \times \cos\theta_j \\ \text{and} \\ x \times \cos\theta_j - y \times \sin\theta_j > X \times \sin\theta_j - Y \times \cos\theta_j \end{array} \right. \right\} \qquad [12]$$

The angle θ_i of a point (x_i, y_i) relative to the center (X, Y) is given by the equations

$$x_i = X + r_i \times \cos \theta_i, \qquad [13]$$

$$y_i = Y + r_i \times \sin \theta_i. \qquad [14]$$

The *circular distance* of an item-point (x_i, y_i) from the j-th radius is defined as:

$$d_i^{AN}(j) = \begin{cases} r_i|\theta_i - \theta_j| & \text{if} & |\theta_i - \theta_j| < \frac{1}{2}\pi \\ r_i|2\pi + \theta_i - \theta_j| & \text{if} & |2\pi + \theta_i - \theta_j| < \frac{1}{2}\pi \\ r_i|\theta_i - \theta_j - 2\pi| & \text{if} & |\theta_i - \theta_j - 2\pi| < \frac{1}{2}\pi \\ \frac{1}{2}\pi r_i & & \text{otherwise} \end{cases} \qquad [15]$$

The loss function for the angular case is now defined by

$$L_{ANGULAR}(X, Y, \theta_1, \ldots, \theta_k) = \sum_{j=1,\ldots,k} \sum_{\substack{(x_i, y_i) \in A_j \\ (x_i, y_i) \notin S_j}} \min[d_i^{AN}(j), d_i^{AN}(j+1)] , \qquad [16]$$

in which S_j is the sector assigned to A_j, namely the one bounded by radii j and $j + 1$. The normalization term for the angular case has been computed to be

$$N_{ANGULAR} = 100 \times 0.15025 \times \frac{n(k-1)}{k} \qquad [17]$$

The separation index for the axial case, then, is

$$\text{ANGULAR SEPRN INDEX} = 1 - \frac{L_{ANGULAR}}{N_{ANGULAR}}. \qquad [18]$$

The Algorithms. The algorithms for minimizing the loss function in each case are based on Powell's method (see Press et al., 1987) and are outlined in Shye (1992).

Regional Hypotheses in Ongoing Research

A Priori Hypotheses and Post-Hoc Partitions

Definitions and data are intimately linked through correspondence hypotheses not only at a particular point in time but they are also related to each other over time in a "partnership" of mutual feedback (Guttman, 1991). The definitions serve to select and structure the observations. The data then lead to modifications, refinements, extensions, and generalizations in the definitional framework. There is no natural beginning of this partnership between data and definitions. Hence, a correspondence between data and definitions can also be established a posteriori. That is, one may recognize certain groupings in the points and then think about a rationale afterward to formulate new hypotheses.

When the definitional framework is complex, one typically does not predict a full-fledged regional system (such as a cylindrex in Figure 11.4) unless past experience leads one to expect such a system. Rather, one uses a more modest strategy with exploratory characteristics and simply tries to partition the space with minimum error and simple partition lines. In SSA, for example, it is common to replace the usual labels of the points in the multidimensional space by the structs of these points on facets *A, B, C,* and so forth, in turn. This yields a facet diagram for each facet and each projection. The distribution of the facet elements then shows if and how the space can be partitioned (see Figure 10.4). Even more liberal, and exploratory, is the attempt to identify space partitions according to new content facets, not conceived in advance. The stability of such partitions, then, is tested in replications.

Replicating Regional Structures

The goodness of the correspondence of a definitional system and a regional structure is evaluated with respect to three criteria: (a) The direct approach is to take into account only what is immediately given—that is, judge the clarity of the correspondence between facets and regions; (b) in addition, one can ask whether the chosen partition of the SSA space accommodates all possible observations that are logically implied by the definitional system; and (3) finally, one should assess the robustness of the structure over replications.

We now turn to this third criterion. Table 7.1 lists several items from the SLF scales. For these items, data were collected for representative German and U.S. samples (Krebs & Schuessler, 1987; Schuessler, 1982). The correlation matrices for the observations are shown in Table 11.3. Obviously, these matrices confirm the first law of attitudes. But do they also reflect the structuples in Table 7.1?

Looking at these matrices through SSA, we find configurations (Figures 11.7 and 11.8) that can both be partitioned in the same radex sense, in which time plays an angular role and environment and modality, respectively, play radial roles. (The figures show the radial regions based on the environment facet only.) The partitions contain few errors, most of them quantitatively minor ones.

Some of these errors relate to ambiguous structuple assignments. For example, Item 11 in Table 7.1 was classified as relating to the present, and this corresponds to the American version; the German wording for this item, in contrast, refers to "feelings during the last few weeks," which involves the (immediate) past. If one thus classifies Item 11 as *past,* one can redraw the boundary lines so that Item 14 falls into the past region where it should fall. Another instance is Item 17, whose classification as affective was based on our understanding of colloquial American language. Its German equivalent seems to be much more cognitive.

Let us now turn to another aspect of the data, the mean scores. In Figures 11.7 and 11.8, we have imported these means into the SSA configurations by making the size of each point proportional to the mean rating of the item it represents. Substantively, larger points indicate a more negative attitude, and so we see that, in both studies, attitudes are more positive toward things that lie in the present and past, and quite negative toward

TABLE 11.3 Correlation Coefficients (Decimal Points Omitted) of SLF Items Described in Table 7.1[a]

	1	2	3	4	5	6	7	8	9	10	11	12	13	14	15	16	17	18	19	20	21	22
1																						
2	12																					
3	20	25																				
4	07	14	28																			
5	11	11	21	18																		
6	07	23	24	13	13																	
7	18	27	36	21	23	34																
8	13	11	29	18	19	11	23															
9	09	10	15	07	16	12	16	10														
10	15	07	12	08	10	06	11	07	03													
11	08	05	12	16	06	04	12	05	05	28												
12	17	17	34	19	15	18	24	12	11	15	19											
13	17	06	22	09	06	03	09	20	10	14	10	18										
14	10	07	16	11	06	06	10	13	08	14	17	22	15									
15	09	05	11	09	06	06	09	11	09	10	13	11	12	20								
16	12	06	12	08	10	06	06	04	15	18	10	12	18	13	01							
17	-02	07	08	08	12	01	10	09	13	09	09	10	01	17	14	12						
18	06	28	29	18	23	30	27	18	15	13	08	23	05	08	01	07	11					
19	14	21	39	16	16	31	08	17	13	14	10	23	10	15	14	08	18	30				
20	02	06	10	08	06	08	06	06	08	15	15	17	07	14	18	06	16	08	14			
21	09	03	16	09	07	06	07	14	14	13	13	23	16	24	22	10	13	06	14	26		
22	04	05	10	15	09	05	03	10	09	08	09	14	06	15	20	06	14	07	10	28	28	
23	06	05	17	18	12	09	14	14	07	19	28	21	10	23	17	11	20	12	13	26	38	35

The following is a lower-triangular matrix (variables 1–23). Each cell gives the German-sample value (upper panel) over the U.S.-sample value (lower panel), as indicated in the note. Values are transcribed as printed.

	1	2	3	4	5	6	7	8	9	10	11	12	13	14	15	16	17	18	19	20	21	22
1																						
2	16																					
3	36	23																				
4	21	14	28																			
5	24	16	27	24																		
6	24	18	34	21	22																	
7	26	18	36	21	25	36																
8	27	10	29	18	20	21	23															
9	24	16	22	18	25	21	22	17														
10	17	06	18	10	13	10	15	14	12													
11	16	03	21	14	08	12	16	14	08	31												
12	24	11	28	18	10	14	22	24	14	16	11											
13	23	09	19	14	12	11	18	20	10	18	15	22										
14	16	05	17	12	07	10	15	12	10	17	15	19	24									
15	15	08	22	12	08	17	17	14	08	14	17	19	20	28								
16	19	10	15	14	16	09	16	14	16	19	18	22	25	19	11							
17	05	08	07	03	07	10	09	04	04	15	18	09	15	20	27	13						
18	27	07	30	27	30	28	25	22	20	12	10	21	13	05	14	16	06					
19	21	20	33	18	18	26	22	18	15	14	14	20	12	19	38	15	22	23				
20	14	14	13	05	06	10	12	12	07	14	13	14	10	11	20	08	15	10	22			
21	11	04	19	10	08	13	16	12	10	26	28	17	21	23	34	17	29	10	29	21		
22	10	05	12	09	04	12	09	09	07	18	20	14	11	13	24	11	19	10	22	13	27	
23	12	05	17	12	10	12	16	12	05	20	18	18	20	19	30	16	31		27	18	36	21

NOTE: a. The upper panel is for the German sample; the lower, for U.S. sample.

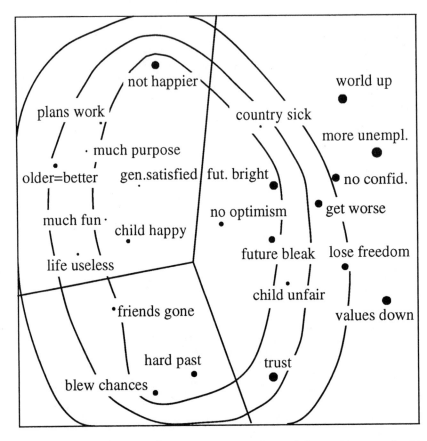

Figure 11.7. SSA Representation of Intercorrelations of German Data on the 23 SLF Items in Table 7.1

NOTE: Partitions are based on structuples in Table 7.1. Point size represents mean item score (large = negative attitude).

the future. A priori, there was no rationale for this finding. Hence, it should generate further thinking about definitional systems that would allow one to predict such a regularity.

Alternative Facetizations

It is sometimes possible to show regional correspondences between the data and different definitional systems for the same set of items. This is

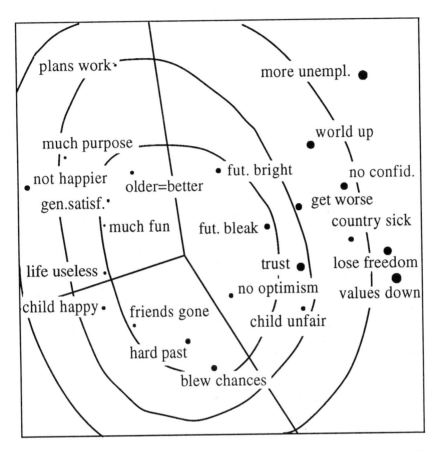

Figure 11.8. SSA Representation of Intercorrelations of U.S. Data on the 23 SLF Items in Table 7.1

NOTE: Partitions are based on structuples in Table 7.1. Point size represents mean item score (large = negative attitude).

particularly useful for checking how alternative theories are related to each other in terms of data. Consider Table 11.2. Borg and Staufenbiel (1993) coded 13 work value items—questions that ask about the importance of different aspects of work—in terms of seven facets. Each of these facets was hypothesized to play an angular or a radial role in the SSA representation.

The facets are based on distinctions made in the work of several prominent researchers in organizational behavior. The interlocking of the facets

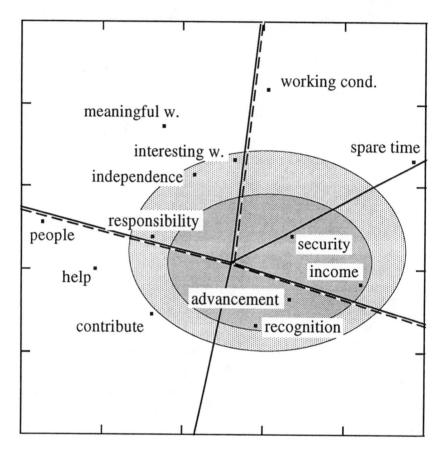

Figure 11.9. SSA Representation of Intercorrelations of 13 Work Values of Table 11.3
NOTE: Partitions were induced by Facets M, R, and L of Table 11.3, respectively.

and the struct assignment of the different items is largely taken directly from previous analyses of these data by others (see Borg, 1991; Borg & Staufenbiel, 1993). Moorhead and Griffin (1989) argue that *security* in Maslow's sense interlocks with both Alderfer's *relatedness* and *existence,* but an item that is both Maslow-type security and Alderfer-type relatedness is missing in our sample of items.

Figure 11.9 shows a two-dimensional SSA representation for the correlations of the 13 work values in a representative German sample. The radex partition is based on the facets $M = Maslow$ (solid radial lines), $R = Rosenberg$ (dashed radial lines) and $L = Levy-Guttman$ (concentric lines).

It is easy to verify—for example, by constructing appropriate facet diagrams—that any other facet in Table 11.2 also induces a perfect and simple partition of this configuration. Moreover, they are all quite similar: The respective regions turn out to be essentially congruent with more or fewer subdivisions. Divergences of the angular partitions are primarily related to the value advancement, which has an ambiguous content anyway (see Chapter 4).

Hence, one concludes that all of these theories are structurally quite similar. This suggests, for example, that Herzberg, Mausner, and Snyderman's (1958) motivation versus hygiene factors relate to the distinction of cognitive versus affective/instrumental values, respectively.

As to the angular facets, we see that the simultaneous partitioning of the SSA space by several circularly ordered facets that are formally not equivalent gives rise to a partial order of the induced sectors. The interlocking of the Herzberg and the Maslow facets implies, for example, that the hygiene region contains the subregions *physiological, security,* and *belongingness,* whereas the *motivators* regions contains *esteem* and *self-actualization.* The subregions, therefore, are forced into a certain neighborhood relation that would not be required without the hierarchical nesting. Similarly, the conceptual interlocking of the Maslow and the Alderfer facet requires esteem to fall between self-actualization and belongingness.

On the Meaning of Regional Patterns

Establishing a correspondence between the cells of the design and regions of a geometrical representation of the data is a nontrivial scientific achievement. However, one rarely stops here by saying *quod erat demonstrandum.* An important further question asks for replicability. But even replicating a regional correspondence, and thereby establishing an empirical law, is not sufficient for science. Researchers typically also want to "understand" the law and, therefore, ask for the "meaning" of the finding. Why, for example, are work values organized in a radex?

An answer to this question can be derived, in part, from reasoning in Shye (1985b, 1989) or Schwarz and Bilsky (1987). The latter authors studied general values. One of the facets they used was *motivational domain* = {achievement, self-direction, security, enjoyment, . . .}. These distinctions were considered nominal ones, but with an additional notion of substantive opposition of some of this facet's elements. Four such oppositions were discussed, for example, achievement versus security:

> To strive for success by using one's skills usually entails both causing some change in the social or physical environment and taking some risks that may

be personally or socially unsettling. This contradicts the concern for preserving the status quo and for remaining psychologically and physically secure that is inherent in placing high priority on security values. (p. 554)

Hence, the region of achievement values was predicted to lie opposite to the security region.

If we use this kind of reasoning post hoc on the work value radex of Figure 11.9, we could "explain" the opposite position of the sector v and a (in Maslow's sense) by a certain notion of "contrast" of striving for self-actualization and for recognition, respectively. This notion of contrast is derived from a basic facet analysis of action systems (Shye, 1985b, 1989). The same facet analysis also explains the neighborhood of regions such as recognition and security.

Searching for Better Facets for Regional Laws

Explanations (or predictions) based on informal reasoning, as in the previous discussion, are a first step toward building a better definitional system. The concentric ordering of *inference, application,* and *learning* in the intelligence cylindrex, for example, has been confirmed in so many studies that further replications become uninteresting. Yet we cannot predict by formal derivation—from the properties of the definitional system, and from the facet {inference, application, learning} in particular— that the regions of inference, application and learning should be ordered this way. This order remains a largely empirical phenomenon. So it becomes natural to ask for modifications of the definitional system that allow such predictions and possibly further testable hypotheses.

Snow, Kyllonen, and Marshalek (1984) suggested an explanation. They report a factor analysis that indicates that items that lie more in the center of the radex (i.e., inference tests) are more "complex" and those at the periphery (such as learning tests) are relatively "specific." But this really only repeats what the radex already expresses (in a more robust way): Items in the radial regions are closer the more one moves toward the center of the radex; hence, the items tend to load higher on the factors that essentially correspond to angular directions (discussed earlier in this chapter). Snow et al. (1984) add, however, that more complex tasks show "increased involvement of one or more centrally important components." Hence, their explanation for the inference-application-learning order seems to be that these facet elements are, in fact, discrete semantic simplifications of a smooth gradient of complexity.

One can ask the complexity question in a different way and define a task $t1$ as more complex than $t2$ if "it requires everything $t1$ does, and more" (Guttman, 1954b, p. 269). Formally, this implies an interlocking of content structuples, analogous to the perfect scale as it applies to score structuples. This requires the identification of basic content facets with a common range, in which the concepts inference, application, and learning become only global labels for comparable (hence ordered) content structuples of these underlying facets. Shye and Klauer (1991) proposed a definitional system that specifies what these "underlying" facets might be.

For a fixed element of the material facet (numerical, verbal, or geometric), such a system would allow one to predict a particular order of regions (simplex). But, then, this leads to the question of what pulls the different simplexes—one for each content verbal, geometrical and numerical, respectively—to a common origin? To explain this requires an additional pattern in the structuples. Formally, for the three directions of the intelligence radex, it would suffice to have an additional coding of the items in terms of the extent to which they address one of the three cognitive tasks (rule inference, application, memory).

Such ideas are further explicated by Guttman (1954b) in parametric form and elucidated by van den Wollenberg (1978). From today's point of view, his developments are very restrictive models of what later developed into the general notions of the radex and regional correspondence hypotheses in general.

Regions and Dimension Systems

Several Axial Facets: The Multiplex

A regionalization always depends on both facets and data. In principle, any simple and replicable regionalization is interesting. Among the many possibilities, the multiplex is a particularly important specimen because it makes clear how partitions are linked to "dimensional interpretations" that are predominant in MDS applications.

Consider an example. Levy (1983) reports a reanalysis of a study on political action by Barnes et al. (1979). She looked at items that assessed attitudes toward political protest behavior, defined as "negative purposeful behavior toward some aspect of society, the purpose being to induce change in that aspect" (p. 284). Three forms of (verbal) attitudinal behavior toward protest acts were distinguished: (a) beliefs on the effectiveness of such acts to bring about the desired change, (b) approval or disapproval of such acts in a normative way, and (c) evaluation of the likelihood of overt protest behavior of the respondent him/herself. A second facet splits protest acts into *demanding* (such as petitions and demonstrations), *obstructive* (such as boycotts and strikes), and physically *damaging* ones (such as violence and political graffiti). A third facet separates protest acts of *omission* from those of *commission*. These combine to form the following mapping sentence:

The ($a1$ = evaluation of effectiveness)
The ($a2$ = approval) behavior of respondent (p)
($a3$ = evaluation of likelihood)
of own overt action

with respect ($b1$ = demanding) ($c1$ = omission)
to a ($b2$ = obstructive) ( ) protest act
($b3$ = physically damaging) ($c2$ = commission)

$\rightarrow$ {*very positive*, . . . , *very negative*} behavior toward protest acts

---

Levy (1983) argues that all three facets are ordered in terms of *strong* to *weak* protest behavior. Except for the order of $a1$ and $a2$, this seems convincing.

Thirty items were selected from the Barnes et al. (1979) studies using this mapping sentence as a culling rule. The structuples for these items are given, together with short verbal labels, in Table 11.4. The range of $a1$-items was *very effective* to *not at all effective; approve strongly* to *disapprove strongly* for $a2$-items; and the facet {have already done in past 10 years, would do, might do in a particular situation, would never do} for $a3$-items. Despite their different wordings, these ranges are just variants of the generic positive-negative range specified in the mapping sentence.

With three ordered facets, an SSA representation of the intercorrelations of the items may be hypothesized to be three-dimensional with each facet playing an axial role. That is, each facet should partition the space into a set of ordered regions. Furthermore, because the mapping sentence does not exclude any structuples, the joint partitioning of all facets is expected to lead to three-dimensional cells for every item type (similar to Figure 4.1). Each structuple therein corresponds to a cell, and those for which there are no data are empty.

Figures 11.10 and 11.11 show that this prediction is almost perfectly satisfied. However, not unexpectedly, Levy's order argument is not con-

TABLE 11.4 Thirty Items of Political Protest, Faceted by A, B, and C[a]

Protest Behavior	a1	a2	a3		
petitions	1	11	21	b1	c2
boycotts	2	12	22	b2	c1
lawful demonstrations	3	13	23	b1	c2
refusing to pay rent	4	14	24	b2	c1
wildcat strikes	5	15	25	b2	c1
painting slogans on walls	6	16	26	b3	c2
occupying buildings	7	17	27	b2	c2
blocking traffic	8	18	28	b2	c2
damaging property	9	19	29	b3	c2
personal violence	10	20	30	b3	c2

NOTES: a. A = {a1 = evaluation of effectiveness, a2 = approval, a3 = evaluation of own overt action}, B = {b1 = demanding, b2 = obstructing, b3 = physically damaging}, and C = {c1 = omission, c2 = commission}; Item 1 has content structuple (a1, b1, c2).

firmed empirically for Facet A: the a1 region lies between the a2 and a3 regions.

Figure 11.12 suggests one way to put together such projection planes. Here, the points are left out not to clutter the graph. This way one can see clearly how the three facets cut the space into boxlike cells. Obviously, the facets act similar to Cartesian dimensions.

Prototypical Partitions and Coordinate Systems

The Cartesian coordinate system is not the only way to coordinate a geometric space. Indeed, the properties of a geometric space do not rely on any coordination, but on the relations on its objects (points, lines, etc.) such as incidence, inclusion, perpendicularity, symmetry, and so forth. Coordinate systems only serve to make these relations accessible to algebra. This is often overlooked in typical MDS applications in which one automatically asks for the meaning of the *dimensions*. It is taken for granted that these dimensions express the essential properties of the geometry, and, moreover, that they can only be Cartesian ones or, in any case, rectilinear ones.

The orthogonal boxlike coordination is the Cartesian method to locate points in *m*-dimensional space. One notes from Figure 11.12 that this corresponds to an *m*-faceted multiplex.

Yet one can also take a cylindrex as a basis for a three-dimensional coordinate system: It is composed of a radex, which corresponds to a polar coordinate system in the plane, and an additional axis protruding ortho-gonally from the radex plane. This gives rise to a cylindrical coordinate

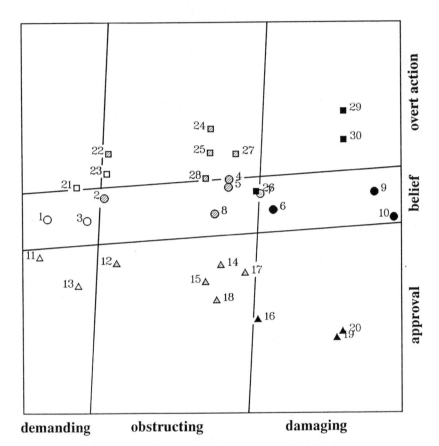

Figure 11.10. Plane Spanned by Two Principal Axes of Three-Dimensional SSA Representation of the Protest Items in Table 11.4

NOTE: Partition was induced by Facets A (y-axis) and B (x-axis).

system, which has been occasionally used in psychophysics. Indow (1974), for example, studied similarity judgments on color chips with structuples (H = hue, V = value, C = chroma) and reported an impressive variety of data sets for which "cylindrical coordinates corresponding to H, V, and C were identified" (p. 502).

Still other coordinate systems are possible. One can generalize, for example, the radex to a spherex by allowing its rays to wander into three-dimensional space. In the limit—with ever more points and ever

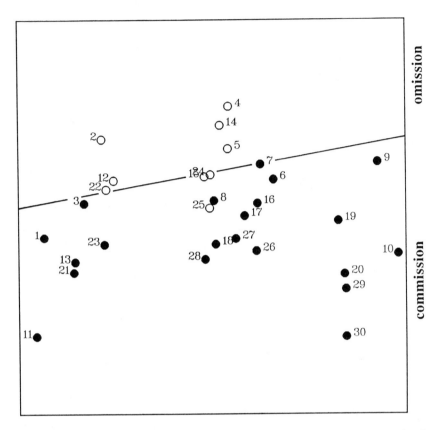

Figure 11.11. Plane Spanned by First (*x*-axis) and Third (*z*-axis) Principal Axis of a Three-Dimensional SSA Representation of the Protest Items in Table 11.4

NOTE: Partitions on the *z*-axis were induced by Facet C.

smaller, ordered regions—this regional system turns into a spherical coordinate system, with one radial and two angular coordinates.

External Variables in SSA

At first glance, the notion of external variables seems foreign to the spirit of FT, because FT favors the integration of all empirical observations into a unified definitional framework. However, scientific investigations often are concerned with relationships between a given content universe

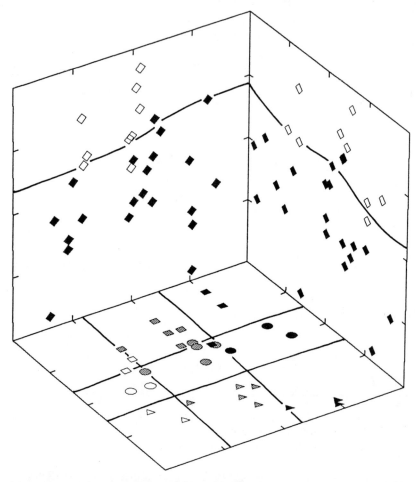

Figure 11.12. Three Principal-Axes Projection Planes of a Three-dimensional SSA Representation of the Protest Items in Table 11.4

NOTE: The partition in the horizontal plane was induced by Facets A (y-axis) and B (x-axis). The partition in the vertical planes was induced by Facet C.

and other variables not (or not yet) in that universe—for external validation or for theoretical explorations, as examples.

A common approach for incorporating an external variable in an SSA simply is to add the external variable to the set of internal variables (items) so that it is represented as a point in the SSA space. But this approach is clearly inadequate: By the FT continuity principle (Shye, 1970; 1991e; Shye & Elizur, 1994), every point in the entire SSA space represents an internal variable—that is, an item (which may or may not have been observed in a particular study) that belongs to the studied content universe. Denesh and Shye (1993), in contrast, proposed an approach based on the notion of *external facets* that, in many ways, parallels the logic of external variables in POSAC (see above). We have seen that a content facet is one that classifies all items in the content universe (i.e., the internal items) and, therefore, can induce a partition on the content universe. In this sense, a content facet may be called an *internal facet*. An external facet, on the other hand, is defined as a classification of the internal items which is specified in terms of the items' properties or "behavior" with respect to a criterion *external to the content universe*. Thus, for example, given an external variable, one may assess its relationship (e.g., compute its correlation) with each one of the content (internal) items. These items, in turn, can be classified according to the strength of their relationship with the external variable.

The external variable defines in effect an external facet on the observed content items. Once an SSA space diagram is produced for the observed content items, one may search for a space partition that would correspond to that external facet. This search can be very instructive and, to the extent a partition induced by an external variable can be related to partitions induced by content facets, it can lead to theoretical insights. In practice, the FSSA program produces, as an option, an "external variable diagram" for each external variable. An external variable diagram is a reproduction of the SSA space diagram, except that instead of an item's ID number, its correlation (monotone or linear) with the external variable is printed, in the same location. Given the external variable diagram, one may try to identify regions of relatively high, medium, or low correlations and explore for possible partition patterns.

In POSAC, an external variable may induce a partition on the POSAC space, in accordance with the relative frequencies of the external trait. Hence, an external variable induces, in effect, a range facet. (This would be, of course, an externally imposed artificial range facet—that is, one that is not necessarily related to the common range of the original content universe.) To see this, simply note that a partition of a POSAC space is equivalent to a mapping of the subjects into a new range. In an analogous way, the procedure for incorporating an external variable into Faceted SSA induces, in effect, an external content facet (not necessarily one from the content universe) on the SSA content space. Two appealing features characterize this procedure: First, the identified partition lines do not depend upon the direction of the range of the external variable—in that reversal of that direction would result in a change of the coefficient signs only. This, again, is in analogy with the POSAC external variable option. Second, the inclusion of an external variable in a particular Faceted SSA does not a priori ensure a well-defined partition pattern. This is an advantage, because, in the course of scientific inquiry, it becomes possible to distinguish between external variables that do induce clear facets and those that do not, thereby stimulating substantive theory.

Regional Hypotheses and Other Statistical Approaches

Regions and Clusters

A number of formal questions arise in discussing regions. One of the most frequent ones concerns the relationship of regions to clusters. As is often true with concepts used in FT relative to similar ones in data analysis, the FT notion is more general. Indeed, region includes cluster as a special case. Lingoes (1981) proposes a faceted way to distinguish among different types of regions. He suggests that a cluster is a particular region whose points are all closer to each other than to any point in some other region. This makes the points in a cluster appear to be packed relatively dense, with empty space around it. For regions, such a requirement is generally not relevant. All they require is a rule that allows one to decide if a point lies within or outside of the region.

Points 5 and 6 in Figure 11.2 are in different regions, but complete linkage clustering, for example, puts them into one cluster together with Point 4, whereas it assigns Points 7 and 8 to another cluster. For regions, the distance of two points—on which clustering is based—does not matter. Indeed, two points can be infinitely close and still be in different regions; conversely, two points may be far apart and yet belong to the same region. All that counts is discriminability. Most important is that clusters are identified on purely technical criteria, whereas regions are derived from the structuples of the points, that is, from content definitions.

Factor Analysis and Regional Hypotheses

One could ask what a factor analysis would uncover for the data in Table 11.4. Principal component analysis with varimax rotation yields three factors with eigenvalues greater than 1. Figure 11.13 shows for the U.S. data how the factors relate to the SSA solution: All points that load highest

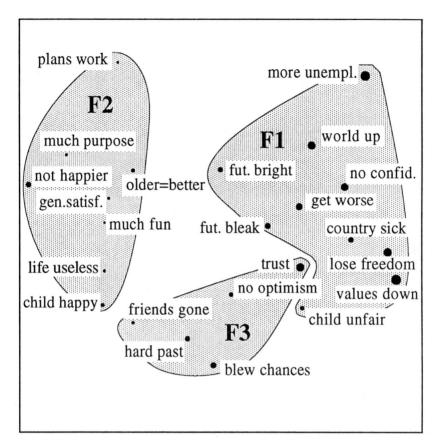

Figure 11.13. SSA Configuration From Figure 11.8 Together With Regions Included by a Factor Analysis of the Same Data

NOTE: Factors explain 13% (F1), 11% (F2), and 8% (F3) of total variance.

on factor F1, F2, or F3, respectively, are collected into the same region. Thus, what we find in this particular example is that our sectors largely correspond to the factors.

This finding is not surprising because of the way in which the SSA distance representation is related to the vector representation of principal component analysis. With positive correlations as we have here, the SSA configuration and the principal component configuration are closely related: In the principal component space, all items are represented by vectors that lie essentially within the positive octant, the projection of their endpoints onto the unit sphere closely resembles the SSA configuration, and the varimax axes are but the Cartesian coordinate axes of the positive octant (Borg & Staufenbiel, 1989; Guttman, 1982a; Shye, 1988). This means, however, that the correspondence of factors and sectors in this case is quite coincidental. Indeed, choosing a rotation other than the varimax yields different relations of factors to regions: The principal axes rotation, for example, leads to a first principal component whose loadings roughly reflect the second facet in Figures 11.7 and 11.8, respectively (see also Snow et al., 1984). Other rotations show no simple correspondence of facet-induced and factor-induced regions.

Generally speaking, one cannot, of course, expect from *any* mechanical approach (such as factor analysis or nonfaceted SSA, for that matter) to automatically come up with a meaningful classification of the points. Looking at factor analysis, in particular, one notes that its factors are very much dependent on the specific distribution of points in space, whereas this is obviously irrelevant for the regional approach. Hence, the latter is not only open-eyed to substance and more flexible with respect to the kind of patterns for which it can account, but also more robust with respect to the particular sampling of items. Item sampling is, however, not irrelevant in SSA either. First, the SSA solution as such obviously depends on the given items. Second, an optimal partitioning generally pays attention to minimizing misclassifications and, thus, weights sparsely sampled items classes less than those represented by a large number of items.

Multitrait-Multimethod and SSA

The multitrait-multimethod (MTMM) approach assesses variables of substantive interest (traits) with different methods. Ostrom (1969), for example, studied attitudes toward the church. He assessed cognitive, affective, and instrumental attitudinal behaviors with four different scaling methods (Thurstone Case-5, Likert, Guttman, direct ratings). The purpose of using such a multiplicity of methods is an attempt to separate substantive from method-induced covariances on the basis of the observed "within" and "between" correlations of the items.

The traits and the methods in MTMM are simply content facets. This view not only helps to systematize the methods in MTMM, but suggests that the *method* is just a facet of the content itself. One can ask how they show up in an SSA representation of the item correlations. Guttman and Levy (1982) report for the Ostrom correlations that they can be organized in a cylindrex, in which the facet {cognitive, affective, instrumental} plays an angular role, and the methods facet plays both a radial and an axial role.

Thus, the methods facet repeats, in a way, the role of the communication facet of the intelligence items in Figure 11.4.

More formally, one notes that the typical MTMM method of comparing correlation coefficients over different combinations of trait and method is compatible with traditional item-analytic principles: What one wants to find or what one wants to construct via item construction/selection is that items of the same content correlate highly over different methods. Regional hypotheses, in contrast, study the discriminability of the items with respect to the facets trait and methods in terms of regional separability. Clustering patterns are considered accidental. To *derive* such clusters or hypotheses on the sizes of correlations, one needs considerably stronger and more differentiated structuples than those that result from a simple trait-method classification.

Structural Equation Modeling and Regional Hypotheses

Structural equation models (LISREL models) attempt to explain the correlations among a battery of variables by some latent factors (such as in factor analysis), but with possibly "causal" relations among these factors (similar to path analysis). Factors and variables are, moreover, conceived as combinations of a true and an error component. The structural model of the latent factors as well as the error model allow for thousands of specifications in a concrete applied context. To be able to identify a solution at all, relatively simple factor structure specifications are set up and simplifying assumptions are made on the errors.

In the FT context, LISREL-like methodology has been used only rarely. The reason ultimately lies in the basic notions of structural equation modeling that are akin to factor and cluster analysis and not to discriminant analysis. That is, LISREL methods ultimately involve a particular case of regional hypotheses that is difficult to derive from structuples or, indeed, from any theoretical conception of the observations.

Consider a paper by Mellenbergh, Keldermann, Stijlen, and Zondag (1979). These researchers studied social fear in children, using two facets, *situations* = {social, intellectual, physical, exclusion, appearance} and *behavior* = {cognitive, avoidance, physiological, affective}. Two sample items are: "During recreation I don't play with other children," with an answering range {*yes, no*}, classified as (social, avoidance); and "Having had a hair cut I am afraid others think I look strange," with the same yes-no range and the structuple (appearance, cognitive).

With these facets—we do not discuss the clarity of their semantics here—Mellenbergh et al. (1979) construct a model. They design various factor structures, with factors based to the structs and different covariance assumptions on the factors. Because a number of models turn out not to be mathematically identifiable, the models are enriched with various technical assumptions that have no relation to the facets. The free parameters are estimated via LISREL.

A number of basic objections can be made against such model estimation practice. For example, De Leeuw (1991) states that

> the stability of the resulting solutions will be doubtful and the usefulness of the detailed aspects of the fitted model even more so. . . . The statistical superstructure is used to sell LISREL to unsuspecting audiences, but it is largely irrelevant and its appropriateness is highly debatable. (p. 243)

Moreover, he continues with the following:

> complicated fitting procedures with many parameters are dangerous techniques, especially if they masquerade as inferential techniques. . . . This type of program appeals greatly to many social scientists who are very unsure about the value of their prior knowledge. They prefer to delegate decisions to the computer, and they expect techniques to generate knowledge. . . . We impose so little prior information on the data, including all outliers, stragglers, idiosyncracies, coding errors, missing data, completely determine the solution. As a consequence results can, of course, never be replicated. (p. 243)

For the moment, disregard statistical inference and the issue of the stability of LISREL solutions over replications. The structural conclusions presented by Mellenbergh et al. (1979) are, in any case, not too revealing: "For the correlation matrix of 20 variables, . . . the following model was used: five situation factors, four reaction factors, and two correlated second-order factors, one a general situation factor and the other a general reaction factor" (p. 775). Expressed geometrically in terms of SSA, this essentially means that the position of a point, for example, for an item of type (exclusion, affective) is approximated by the centroid of the exclusion points and the centroid of the affective points. That is, what LISREL model builders look for is a closeness relation—such as in factor or cluster analysis—instead of a discriminant function as in regional hypotheses (Denison, 1982). It is taken for granted, a priori, that the situation and the behavior types form clusters. The rationale for this assumption is not explicated but probably comes close to the rationale that "underlies" the contiguity principle.

One notes, furthermore, that Mellenbergh et al.'s (1989) final model does not contain causal elements. Such an element is represented by a single-headed arrow from one factor to other factors. The former is then taken as the "cause" of the latter. Technically, it is easy to set up such hypotheses, but to find a rationale for it or to be actually able to derive it from properties of the definitional framework, seems exceedingly difficult, except in special cases in which, for example, a time facet is involved.

Note

1. What would be desirable in a FT context, in which each point is associated with a particular structuple, is an SSA which minimizes Stress under the additional constraint that the points be placed such that the space can be optimally partitioned into regions, facet by facet (similar to MSA). Such a procedure, requiring the definition of a multivalued loss function, was outlined by Guttman (1976), but not studied further or programmed.

Some Concluding Comments on FT

- FT and Measurement Theory
- Arguments Against FT
- Mapping Sentence Definitions
- Purposiveness of Facets
- FT and Significance Testing
- FT and Rigorous Science
- "Complexity" of FT Results and Indexes
- FT and Hard Sciences
- Standard Steps of a FT-Driven Project

FT and Measurement Theory

Facet theory (FT) is often associated with measurement or data analysis in the social sciences. This notion is not incorrect but is too narrow and too vague. In that considerable confusion arises from the term *measurement* itself, it seems useful to first distinguish different definitions of measurement. In the literature, one finds, implicitly or explicitly, at least four. (Borg & Staufenbiel, 1989). We can skip two of them because they are either completely application oriented and geared only at external validity (index measurement; see Dawes, 1972) or because they study formal representational issues similar to fundamental measurement (derived measurement; Schönemann & Borg, 1983; Suppes & Zinnes, 1963).

The two versions left are *fundamental measurement* (FM) and *measurement as structural theory* (MST). FM is dominated by measurement theory that strives to characterize mathematically the properties of prototypical empirical relational systems that can be represented by similar numerical systems. FM theory is, thus, largely a matter for mathematicians. Luce (personal communication), responding to a critical article by Schönemann (1994), states that "FM is fundamentally a mathematical development in which data are presented as illustrative, not as systematic presentation of empirical theory." Social scientists are supposed to serve themselves with models, but they face the problem of how to select and how to interpret the models.

MST hinges on the notion that measurement is always done with a substantive purpose (Guttman, 1971). MST underscores that measurement itself—the assignment of numerical value(s) to an object (e.g., person) with respect to an attribute (e.g., intelligence)—rests heavily, if not always explicitly, on assumptions concerning the structure of the attribute and, hence, on a theory one holds true. Take, for example, the simplest case of the Guttman scale as a measuring device. A Guttman scale is first and foremost a hypothesis on the correspondence between a content (i.e., observational items drawn therefrom) and the order relations among the observed data structuples: That is, these structuples all should be comparable. More concretely, given a content universe U in sample G, say, the Guttman scale hypothesis anticipates that out of the $2^4 = 16$ possible structuples only the following 5 can be observed:

Guttman Scale Structuples	Assigned Score
0000	1
1000	2
1100	3
1110	4
1111	5

If such a scale is repeatedly confirmed (and not refuted) in replication, it becomes a theory on which a single score ordinal assessment can be based (assigned score). If it is refuted, no such measurement can be reasonably made and one needs to try partial order scalogram analysis (see Chapter 10). A Guttman scale, when confirmed, is associated with a very simple content space. In fact, its SSA content space (based on monotone correlations of the columns of the scalogram) is simply one point (zero-dimensional space). This corresponds well with the fact that attributes that can be assessed by a Guttman scale are indeed monolithic—are not differentiated into finer aspects by empirically validated content facets.

In the behavioral sciences, Guttman scales are rare. Therefore, we often resort to POSAC/LSA. Two-dimensional scalograms may correspond to one- or two-dimensional content spaces, depending on the actual configuration of the observed scalogram. Hence, FT-based MST points to a formal and explicated way of showing how the measurement of observed objects is related to a structural theory of the attribute.

Comparing FM and MST, one notes that the main asset of FM models lies in the detailed error diagnostic they provide. This can serve further model refinement and is often the main purpose of FM users (see, e.g., Luce, 1989). Yet this does not contradict the MST approach, because MST-based research is obviously not merely "descriptive": Rather, it systematically tests correspondences of definitional systems to observations. In that definitional systems can become quite technical and formalized, one notes that the basic difference between FM and MST does not lie in formalism or falsifiability issues, but in the strategic decision to work top-down from a fully developed formal model or, alternatively, bottom-up from defining and facetizing a particular substantive universe of items.

Arguments Against FT

Bohrnstedt (personal communication), in a recent symposium on attitude measurement, remarked that FT, to a substantial degree, is but a design methodology. He then asked if anybody was "against" design. No answer, of course, is needed. As a design methodology, FT is not controversial. One can discuss, however, if a top-down approach (as in FM) or a bottom-up approach (as in MST) is ultimately the better strategy. Yet this is not so much a theoretical question as it is an empirical one. To some extent, it is also naive, because it assumes that scientists work only this way or that way. Most, if not all, scientists do not subscribe to a particular methodology in practice. Rather, they take advantage of anything that seems useful at the moment, be it exploration or top-down model building. How one sells the findings to the audiene in the end is a different matter. In that FT is a strategy that has been found to be useful and successful in different ways and in various substantive contexts, there is no reason for an opportunistic researcher not to make use of it. This is even more true because FT can complement and integrate many other methodologies.

Mapping Sentence Definitions

Mapping sentence definitions are based on mapping definitions (see Chapter 7), but they specify content facets that render the definition more "operational." Even if one makes no further use of FT at all, such mapping definition sentences can be extremely practical.

Consider a case. On a recent symposium on payment and reward systems in industrial organizations, the discussants began to run into serious communication problems because of the multiplicity of terms that were used in this context. It remained unclear to what extent these terms meant the same things or in which ways they differed or were supposed to differ. Such facets of distinction can be explicated in a sentence such as the following (after Borg & Bergermaier, 1992):

```
The extent to which (p) receives a

                                              Values
                                          (   advancement   )
                                          (   freedom       )
  (   systematic   )                      (   information   )
  (                )  allocation of       (   power         )   through
  (   ad hoc       )  resources in area   (   prestige      )
                                          (   money         )
                                          (   security      )

                                    Reward Criterion
                                  (   individual performance   )
     Allocator                    (   collective performance   )
  (   organization   )            (   position, role           )
  (   supervisor     )            (   need                     )
  (   work team      )  on the    (   seniority                )   in
  (   coworkers      )  basis of  (   equality                 )
  (   ...            )            (   working conditions        )
                                  (   unspecified              )

                          Goal
                  (   justice                  )
                  (   collective performance   )
                  (   individual performance   )        (  high  )
  order to        (   commitment               )   →    (  ...   )   resource allocation
  achieve         (   entrance to organization )        (  low   )
                  (   legal requirements       )
                  (   unspecified              )
```

This definition can be easily extended, and it can be made more interesting by ordering the facets conceptually and rephrasing some of them in more abstract terms (Levy & Guttman, 1981). Whether this should be done depends on the context. For coordinating key concepts in a conference, one should not diverge too far from the language that is used by most.

Purposiveness of Facets

Facets are always defined to serve a particular purpose. A new object of interest, in the beginning, is seen monolithically, and then facets are invented and tested for their empirical validity to gain conceptual and empirical control. Similarities and distinctions thus are pointed out, but universal classifications are impossible because what is useful in one context may be irrelevant in another. Guttman (1991), accordingly, asks whether the Mendeleev system or the earth-air-fire-water typology is "better." In that a decision requires one to specify a *for what,* one notes that there is no simple answer. That does not mean, of course, that there cannot exist facets with a wide range of applications. Yet even they are not universal.

FT and Significance Testing

A frequent argument against FT is that it does not make use of inferential statistics, even though such tests are not impossible to construct in a FT-oriented data analytic approach (see, e.g., Lingoes, 1983; Lingoes & Cooper, 1971). As with most model builders in the FM sense, FT researchers follow a strategy of successive approximation, advancing from replication to replication with definitional systems (models) that describe the data ever more precisely.

With this neglect of inferential statistics, FT finds itself in respectable company. Meehl (1978, 1981), for example, argues as follows:

> I suggest to you that Sir Ronald has befuddled us, mesmerized us, and led us down the primrose path. I believe that the universal reliance on merely refuting the null hypothesis as the standard method for corroborating substantive theories in the soft areas is a terrible mistake, is basically unsound, poor scientific strategy, and one of the worst things that ever happened in the history of psychology. (p. 256)

Similar arguments are made by Luce (1989):

> Psychology is one of the heavier consumers of statistics. Presumably the reason is that psychologists have become convinced that they are greatly aided

in making correct scientific inferences by casting their decision making into the framework of statistical inference. In my view, we have witnessed a form of mass deception of the sort typified by the story of the emperor with no clothes. Statistical inference techniques are good for what they were developed for, mostly making decisions about the probable success of agriculture, industrial, and drug interventions, but they are not especially appropriate to scientific inference which, in the final analysis, is trying to model what is going on, not merely to decide if one variable affects another. What has happened is that many psychologists have forced themselves into thinking in a way dictated by inferential statistics, not by the problems they really wish or should wish to solve. (p. 281)

Further and detailed arguments against using inferential statistics in scientific research can also be found in Carver (1978), De Leeuw (1994), Guttman (1977, 1985b), Tukey (1988), among others. If one draws a conclusion from their writings, the least would be that significance tests are, at best, of rather secondary importance for cumulative theory construction.

FT and Rigorous Science

FT-based hypotheses (such as regional hypotheses, for example), often appear to be quite soft, and hard to falsify. Sometimes they are believed to be more akin to projective tests than to rigorous science. We have, however, already shown earlier that this impression is not correct. Partitionability hypotheses are usually stronger than, for example, traditional discriminant hypotheses, because they do not allow for overlapping distributions. Moreover, one typically does not predict just "some" partition, but rather a particular pattern of regions that should also be replicable, valid for all items in the universe, and open for further refinement.

We saw in Chapter 11 how difficult it may be to provide simple answers to complex questions. Shye's (1991a) Faceted SSA for partitioning an SSA space by a priori facets adds further rigor to the regional hypotheses. The facet separation index provided by FSSA gives a measure of the scientific significance of an aspect of the tested theory. The theory, of course, also has to be evaluated by additional criteria that require one to look beyond what can be tested on the particular sample of data.

Yet FT researchers typically avoid exceedingly rigorous tests and, thus, are willing to live with certain risks. They are, in this sense, in agreement with Tukey (1987), who believes that pseudoscience operates on principles such as, "be simple, very simple . . . be exactly wrong, rather than approximately right . . . beware empiricism, it isn't scientific . . . at all costs be rigid and serious" (p. 199).

"Complexity" of FT Results and Indexes

Most FT applications so far have been scientific in nature. Thus, the question of what one could *do* with a result such as the intelligence cylindrex, for example, is really irrelevant.

Psychologists often ask for indexes. For example, they look at the intelligence cylindrex and criticize FT for not telling them how to use it for constructing an index and then turn to factor analysis because its mechanical rigidity makes life look simple. In contrast, in a FT approach, we would first systematically ask, Index for what? and set up a faceted goal structure (Borg, 1993b). The purpose might be, for example, to predict job performance, and so one would start by looking closely at the facets *predict, job,* and *performance,* and their relationships. This is likely to lead to a relatively complex system that could then be linked to the equally complex system *intelligence.* How one deals with this complexity (e.g., by abstraction, by controlling certain facets, or by simplification) is an important design question, but it is certainly not FT's fault that the world is complex.

As a next step, FT suggests that we look at the data from the perspective of partial order scalogram analysis and, by using POSAC/LSA, derive a reasonably small number of scales commensurate with the complexity of the studied universe. This results in multiple scaling, which provides a theoretically justified basis for an index or, more commonly, a set of indexes (Shye, 1985a). This approach has been applied successfully, for example, for constructing indexes for the quality of life of individuals and populations (Municipality of Jerusalem, 1992; Shye, 1989); for evaluating environmental projects (Shye, 1982); for assessing focal concerns of declarations and charters on the rights of children (Veerman, 1992); and for evaluating cures in institutions (Wozner, 1982, 1991).

As another example, consider the work value radex in Figure 11.9. If one wants indexes for the importance of work based on the 13 work values assessed here, then the radex suggests different possibilities: (a) Aggregate over all 13 work values to obtain one single index; (b) aggregate over the work values that correspond to different structuples or regions of the radex to obtain six indexes (for Elizur's system of two facets with two and three structs, respectively); or (c) finally, if six indexes are too many, one may opt for four indexes, three that combine "no performance dependency" with one element from the facet {affective, cognitive, instrumental}, and a fourth index that combines all measurements that are "performance dependent" by definition because of their high empirical similarity. Building indexes in such a way is open-eyed, content-oriented, and also based on a verified correspondence hypothesis between conceptual and empirical structure. Factor-analytical approaches, in contrast, are typically based only on a particular aspect of the data.

FT and Hard Sciences

The illustration and cases that we discussed in this book were taken mostly from the soft disciplines of the social sciences. We chose them because they appeal to the largest audience and because it is the soft areas in which progress seems most difficult to achieve. FT, however, is not restricted to such areas. We saw how, for the Hull-Spence learning models, a mapping sentence, through formalization of its language, can be gradually developed into a mathematical model.

Any systematic research, in any case, is implicitly facet-theoretical. Rothkopf (1958), for example, studied confusion probabilities of Morse code signals. Such signals are acoustical events that consist of short and long signals and pauses in between. Their physical properties automatically define a structuple whose facets are reflected, in multiple ways, in confusion data (Borg & Lingoes, 1987; Wish, 1965). Similar to verbal items, physical stimuli can also be characterized in more than just one way. Borg and Leutner (1983), for example, studied the perception of simple geometrical stimuli. The rectangles they use can be objectively described not only by height and width but also by area and shape. However, if one assumes a simple composition rule of these facets for similarity judgments, and thus moves into a mathematical model, the height-width facetization allows explanation of the data with less error.

Many more examples of using FT in hard(er) areas could be discussed here. Rather than presenting more, we would like to conclude with one comment. In the hard(er) disciplines of the behavioral sciences, one occasionally finds a situation that features full-fledged mathematical models and sophisticated experiments on one side, but only vague definitions of the universe of discourse on the other. This often leads to undisciplined generalizations of findings established under special experimental conditions to, say, "behavior" in general (as, e.g., in the Hull-Spence example discussed earlier). A differentiated mapping sentence with substantively explicated facets and not just formal place holders could serve to introduce control in this direction. Formulating such mapping sentences in no way restricts data analysis or model building.

Standard Steps of a FT-Driven Project

Abstract and philosophical discussions about methodology may be interesting to read, but they offer little that is of practical use for the substantively oriented scientist. Thus, to conclude, let us return to a very practical level by outlining standard steps of a FT research. Even though such a listing necessarily remains somewhat simplistic and sterile, it may nevertheless serve as a useful guide for the novice.

Provided that a question is given that cannot be solved by formal means but that requires an answer from Nature, a FT-driven approach for seeking an answer essentially involves five steps:

1. Formulate the research question as a hypothesis about a correspondence of a definitional system and an aspect of pertinent observations, together with a rationale for the correspondence.
2. Specify and structure the definitional system in detail:
   • define the population P
   • define the item universe (Q and R)
   • study common range(s) of items
   • distinguish among item types within the universe (facetize)
   • clarify semantics and roles of facets—build mapping sentence(s)
   • construct or cull concrete items
3. Collect pertinent data.
4. Analyze data by studying the correspondences of aspects of the data to the definitional system.
5. Extend, generalize, and specify the findings:
   • add facets and elements within facets
   • further constrain facets (e.g., turning qualitative facets into ordered ones)
   • drop or replace facets
   • increase the level of formality of mapping sentence(s)
   • further specify correspondence hypotheses

Step 2 is particularly complex. In practice, it involves an interplay of articulating facets and mapping sentences on the one hand and formulating concrete items on the other. Items often serve as "tests" of the clarity, completeness, and reliability of initial mapping sentences. That is, given a mapping sentence, formulating or culling items that satisfy this mapping sentence often shows in what areas the mapping sentence is still deficient: Some facets may be too ambiguous, other facets may be missing, the semantics of the mapping sentence may be incomplete or twisted, and so on. Consequently, concrete items are difficult to characterize in terms of the mapping sentence; structuple assignments become vague and debatable. In that case, more work has to be invested into improving the mapping sentence and its facets. Hence, it is usually helpful to test some concrete items after developing an initial mapping sentence and then alternate between work on the mapping sentence and formulating concrete items together with their structuples.

In practice, it is typical that one does not approach a field from scratch. Items already exist from other research, and it is useful to begin by dissecting these items for the facets they contain and setting up an initial mapping sentence on that basis.

In addition to such partnerships within a step, the five steps outlined are not meant, of course, to suggest that facet-theory driven research is a linear process. Rather, as pointed out repeatedly throughout this text, there is a mutually constraining partnership (theory) between aspects of the definitional system and aspects of the empirical observations.

References

Alderfer, C. P. (1972). *Existence, relatedness, and growth: Human needs in organizational settings.* New York: Free Press.

Anastasi, A. (1983). Evolving trait concepts. *American Psychologist, 38,* 175-184.

Aschoff, R. L., Gupta, S. K., & Minas, J. S. (1962). *Scientific method: Optimizing applied research decisions.* New York: John Wiley.

Atkinson, J. W. (1964). *An introduction to motivation.* Princeton, NJ: Van Nostrand.

Barnes, S. H., Kaase, M., Klaus, R., Allerbeck, K., Farah, B. G., Heunks, F., Inglehart, R., Jennings, M. K., Klingeman, H. D., Marsh, A., & Rosenmeyer, L. (Eds.). (1979). *Political action: Mass participation in five western democracies.* Beverly Hills, CA: Sage.

Bastide, R., & van den Berghe, P. (1957). Stereotypes, norms and interracial behavior. *American Sociological Review, 22,* 689-694.

Bentler, P. M., & Weeks, D. G. (1978). Restricted multidimensional scaling models. *Journal of Mathematical Psychology, 17,* 138-151.

Bloombaum, M. (1968). The conditions underlying riots as portrayed by multidimensional scalogram analysis: A reanalysis of Lieberson and Silverman's data. *American Sociological Review, 33,* 76-91.

Borg, I. (1977). Some basic concepts of facet theory. In J. C. Lingoes (Ed.), *Geometric representations of relational data* (pp. 65-102). Ann Arbor, MI: Mathesis Press.

Borg, I. (1986a). A cross-cultural replication on Elizur's facets of work values. *Multivariate Behavioral Research, 21,* 401-410.

Borg, I. (1986b). Facettentheorie: Prinzipien und Beispiele. [Facet theory: Principles and examples.] *Psychologische Rundschau, 37,* 121-137.

Borg, I. (1991). Multiple facetizations of work values. *Applied Psychology: An International Review, 39,* 401-412.

Borg, I. (1992). *Grundlagen und Ergebnisse der Facettentheorie*. [Foundations and results of facet theory.] Bern, Switzerland: Huber.

Borg, I. (1993a). Facet theory: A systematic approach to linking theoretical reasoning to survey research. In W. Bilsky, C. Pfeiffer, & P. Wetzels (Eds.), *Fear of crime and criminal victimization* (pp. 99-128). Stuttgart, Germany: Enke.

Borg, I. (1993b, August-September). How to construct indices in facet theory. *Proceedings of the Fourth International Facet Theory Conference, Prague* (pp. 30-37). Jerusalem, Israel: Facet Theory Association.

Borg, I. (1994). Evolving notions of facet theory. In I. Borg & P. Ph. Mohler (Eds.), *Trends and perspectives in empirical social research* (pp. 178-200). New York: Walter DeGryuter.

Borg, I. (1994). Facet theory. In R. J. Sternberg (Ed.), *Encyclopedia of intelligence* (pp. 419-422). New York: Macmillan.

Borg, I., & Bergermaier, R. (1992). Leistungserbringung: Über die Wichtigkeit der nicht-monetären Bestandteile der Entlohnung. [High performance: On the importance of the non-monetary reward components] In *Entlohnung in der Praxis* (pp. 115-126). Ann Arbor, MI: Mathesis Press.

Borg, I., & Galinat, W. (1986). Struktur und Verteilung von Arbeitswerten. [Structure and distribution of work values.] *Psychologische Beiträge, 28*, 495-515.

Borg, I., & Leutner, D. (1983). Dimensional models for the perception of rectangles. *Perception and Psychophysics, 34*, 257-269.

Borg, I., & Lingoes, J. C. (1980). A model and algorithm for multidimensional scaling with external constraints on the distances. *Psychometrika, 45*, 25-38.

Borg, I., & Lingoes, J. C. (1987). *Multidimensional similarity structure analysis*. New York: Springer.

Borg, I., & Noll, H. H. (1990). Wie wichtig ist "wichtig"? [How important is "important"?] *ZUMA Nachrichten, 14*, 36-48.

Borg, I., Scherer, K., & Staufenbiel, T. (1986). Determinanten von Peinlichkeit und Scham: Ein facettentheoretischer Ansatz. [Determinants of embarrassment and shame: A facet-theoretical approach.] *Archiv für Psychologie, 138*, 53-70.

Borg, I., & Staufenbiel, T. (1989). *Theorien und Methoden der Skalierung*. [Theories and methods of scaling.] Bern, Switzerland: Huber.

Borg, I., & Staufenbiel, T. (1993). Facet theory and design for attitude measurement and its application. In D. Krebs & P. Schmidt (Eds.), *New directions in attitude measurement* (pp. 206-237). New York: Walter DeGryuter.

Borg, I., Staufenbiel, T., & Scherer, K. (1987). On the symbolic basis of pride and shame: A facet theoretical approach. In K. Scherer (Ed.), *Facets of emotion: Recent research* (pp. 79-98). Hillsdale, NJ: Lawrence Erlbaum.

Brody, N. (1988). *Personality: In search of individuality*. New York: Academic Press.

Brown, J. (1985). An introduction to the uses of facet theory. In D. Canter (Ed.), *Facet theory: Approaches to social research* (pp. 17-57). New York: Springer.

Canter, D. (1985). *Facet theory: Approaches to social research*. New York: Springer.

Carver, R. P. (1978). The case against statistical significance testing. *Harvard Educational Review, 48*, 378-399.

Cliff, N. (1983). Evaluating Guttman scales: Some old and new thoughts. In H. Wainer & S. Messick (Eds.), *Principals of modern psychological measurement: A festschrift for Frederic M. Lord* (pp. 283-301). Hillsdale, NJ: Lawrence Erlbaum.

Coombs, C. H. (1983). *Psychology and mathematics: An essay on theory*. Ann Arbor: University of Michigan Press.

Coombs, C. H., Dawes, R. M., & Tversky, A. (1970). *Mathematical psychology: An elementary introduction*. Englewood Cliffs, NJ: Prentice Hall.

Coombs, C. H., & Smith, J. E. K. (1973). On the detection of structure in attitudes and developmental processes. *Psychological Review, 80,* 273-351.

Cronbach, L. J. (1971). *Essentials of psychological testing.* New York: Harper & Row.

Dancer, L. S. (1986). *Facet analysis of suicidal behavior.* Doctoral dissertation. Austin: University of Texas.

Dancer, L. S (1990a). Introduction to facet theory and its applications. *Applied Psychology: An International Review, 39,* 365-377.

Dancer, L. S. (1990b). Suicide prediction and the partial order scalogram analysis of psychological adjustment. *Applied Psychology: An International Review, 39,* 479-497.

Davison, M. L. (1983). *Multidimensional scaling.* New York: John Wiley.

Dawes, R. M. (1972). *Fundamentals of attitude measurement.* New York: John Wiley.

De Leeuw, J. (1991). Data modeling and theory construction. In J. J. Hox & J. DeJong-Gierveld (Eds.), *Operationalization and research strategy* (pp. 229-246). Amsterdam: Swets & Zeitlinger.

De Leeuw, J. (1994). Statistics and the sciences. In I. Borg & P. Ph. Mohler (Eds.), *Trends and perspectives in the empirical social sciences* (pp. 131-148). New York: Walter DeGryuter.

De Leeuw, J., & Heiser, W. J. (1977). Convergence of correction matrix algorithms for multidimensional scaling. In J. C. Lingoes, E. Roskam, & I. Borg (Eds.), *Geometric representations of relational data* (pp. 735-752). Ann Arbor, MI: Mathesis Press.

De Leeuw, J., & Heiser, W. J. (1980). Multidimensional scaling with restrictions on the configuration. In P. R. Krishnaiah (Ed.), *Multivariate analysis* (Vol. 5, pp. 501-522). Amsterdam: North-Holland.

Denesh, I., & Shye, S. (1993, August-September). Facet-inducing external variables: A new FSSA procedure. *Proceedings of the Fourth International Facet Theory Conference, Prague* (pp. 79-87). Jerusalem, Israel: Facet Theory Association.

Denison, D. R. (1982). Multidimensional scaling and structural equation modeling: A comparison of multivariate techniques for theory testing. *Multivariate Behavioral Research, 17,* 447-470.

Elizur, D. (1984). Facets of work values. *Journal of Applied Psychology, 69,* 379-389.

Elizur, D., Borg, I., Hunt, R., & Magyari-Beck, I. (1991). The structure of work values: A cross cultural comparison. *Journal of Organizational Behavior, 12,* 21-38.

Eysenck, H. J. (1979). *The structure and measurement of intelligence.* New York: Springer-Verlag.

Fischer, G. (1990). Conference paper. *New directions in attitude measurement.* Bad Homburg, Germany.

Fishburn, P. C. (1964). *Decision and value theory.* New York: John Wiley.

Fishburn, P. C. (1970). *Utility theory for decision making.* New York: John Wiley.

Foa, U. (1965). New developments in facet design and analysis. *Psychological Review, 72,* 262-274.

Foa, U. G. (1958). The contiguity principle in the structure of interpersonal relations. *Human Relations, 11,* 229-238.

Galinat, W., & Borg, I. (1987). On symbolic temporal information: Beliefs about the experience of duration. *Memory & Cognition, 15,* 308-317.

Gower, J. C. (1985). Measures of similarity, dissimilarity, and distance. In S. Kotz & N. L. Johnson (Eds.), *Encyclopedia of statistical sciences* (Vol. 5, pp. 397-405). New York: John Wiley.

Gratch, H. (Ed.). (1973). *Twenty-five years of social research in Israel.* Jerusalem: Jerusalem Academic Press.

Graumann, C. F. (1994). A phenomenological approach to social research: The perspective of the other. In I. Borg & P. Ph. Mohler (Eds.), *Trends and perspectives in empirical social research* (pp. 283-293). New York: Walter DeGryuter.

Green, B. F. (1954). Attitude measurement. In G. Lindzey (Ed.), *Handbook of social psychology*. Reading, MA: Addison Wesley.

Groenen, P. J. F. (1994). *The majorization approach to multidimensional scaling*. Leiden, Netherlands: DSWO Press.

Guilford, J. P. (1967). *The nature of human intelligence*. New York: McGraw-Hill.

Guttman, L. (1944). A basis for scaling qualitative data. *American Sociological Review, 9,* 139-150. (Reprinted in *Louis Guttman on theory and methodology: Selected writings,* pp. 211-222, by S. Levy, Ed., Aldershot, UK: Dartmouth)

Guttman, L. (1954a). An outline of some new methodology for social research. *Public Opinion Quarterly, 18,* 395-404.

Guttman, L. (1954b). A new approach to factor analysis: The radex. In P. F. Lazarsfeld (Ed.), *Mathematical thinking in the social sciences* (pp. 258-348). New York: Free Press.

Guttman, L. (1954c). The principal components of scalable attitudes. In P. F. Lazarsfeld (Ed.), *Mathematical thinking in the social sciences* (pp. 216-257). New York: Free Press.

Guttman, L. (1959a). Introduction to facet design and analysis. *Proceedings of the Fifteenth International Congress of Psychology, Brussels—1957* (pp. 130-132). Amsterdam: North Holland.

Guttman, L. (1959b). A structural theory for intergroup beliefs and action. *American Sociological Review, 24,* 318-328.

Guttman, L. (1965a). A faceted definition of intelligence. In R. Eifermann (Ed.), *Studies in psychology (Scripta Hierosolymitana, XIV)* (pp. 166-181). Jerusalem: Magnes Press.

Guttman, L. (1965b). The structure of interrelations among intelligence tests. In C. W. Harris (Ed.), *Proceedings of the 1964 Invitational Conference on Testing Problems* (pp. 25-36). Princeton, NJ: Educational Testing Service. (Reprinted in *Louis Guttman on theory and methodology: Selected writings,* pp. 135-146, by S. Levy, Ed., Aldershot, UK: Dartmouth)

Guttman, L. (1968). A general nonmetric technique for finding the smallest coordinate space for a configuration of points. *Psychometrika, 33,* 469-506.

Guttman, L. (1970). Integration of test design and analysis. In *Toward a theory of achievement measurement—Proceedings of the 1969 Invitational Conference on Testing Problems* (pp. 53-65). Princeton, NJ: Educational Testing Service.

Guttman, L. (1971). Measurement as structural theory. *Psychometrika, 36,* 329-347.

Guttman, L. (1972). A partial-order scalogram classification of projective techniques. In M. Hammer, K. Salzinger, & S. Sutton (Eds.), *Psychopathology* (pp. 481-490). New York: John Wiley.

Guttman, L. (1976, November). *Faceted SSA-I.* Unpublished manuscript.

Guttman, L. (1977). What is not what in statistics. *The Statistician, 26,* 81-107. (Reprinted in *Louis Guttman on theory and methodology: Selected writings,* pp. 277-303, by S. Levy, Ed., Aldershot, UK: Dartmouth)

Guttman, L. (1978, August). *Recent structural laws of human behavior.* Paper presented at the Ninth International Sociological Congress. Uppsala, Sweden.

Guttman, L. (1982a). Facet theory, smallest space analysis, and factor analysis. *Perceptual and Motor Skills, 54,* 491-493.

Guttman, L. (1982b, March). *Principal components of attitudes.* Unpublished handout. University of Chicago, Department of Psychiatry.

Guttman, L. (1982c, June). *Scientific concepts and their primacy levels.* Unpublished handout. Hebrew University of Jerusalem.

Guttman, L. (1982d, March). *Some intrinsic models for data analysis.* Unpublished handout. University of Chicago, Department of Statistics.

Guttman, L. (1982e). What is not what in theory construction. In R. Hauser, D. Mechanic, & A. Haller (Eds.), *Social structure and behavior* (pp. 331-347). New York: Academic Press. (Reprinted, with minor changes, from *Multidimensional data representations: When and why,* pp. 47-64, by I. Borg, Ed., 1981, Ann Arbor, MI: Mathesis Press.)

Guttman, L. (1983, February). A mapping sentence for observations on individual social behavior. Unpublished handout. University of Chicago, Department of Psychiatry.

Guttman, L. (1985a). Coefficients of polytonicity and monotonicity. In S. Kotz & N. L. Johnson (Eds.), *Encyclopedia of statistical sciences* (Vol. 7, pp. 80-87). New York: John Wiley.

Guttman, L. (1985b). The illogic of statistical inference for cumulative science. *Applied Stochastic Models and Data Analysis, 1,* 3-10. (Reprinted in *Louis Guttman on theory and methodology: Selected writings,* pp. 341-347, by S. Levy, Ed., Aldershot, UK: Dartmouth)

Guttman, L. (1985c). Multidimensional structuple analysis (MSA-I) for the classification of cetacea: Whales, porpoises and dolphins. In J.-F. Marcotorchino, J.-M. Proth, & J. Jansen (Eds.), *Data analysis in real life environment: Ins and outs of solving problems* (pp. 45-53). (Reprinted in *Louis Guttman on theory and methodology: Selected writings,* pp. 265-273, by S. Levy, Ed., Aldershot, UK: Dartmouth)

Guttman, L. (1988). ETA, DISCO, ODISCO, and F. *Psychometrika, 53,* 393-405.

Guttman, L. (1991). *Louis Guttman: In Memoriam—Chapters from an unfinished textbook on facet theory.* Jerusalem: Israel Academy of Sciences and Humanities.

Guttman, L. (1992). The irrelevance of factor analysis for the study of group differences. *Multivariate Behavioral Research, 27,* 175-204.

Guttman, L., & Levy, S. (1982). On the definition and varieties of attitude and wellbeing. *Social Indicators Research, 10,* 159-174. (Reprinted in *Louis Guttman on theory and methodology: Selected writings,* pp. 21-36, by S. Levy, Ed., Aldershot, UK: Dartmouth)

Guttman, L., & Levy, S. (1991). Two structural laws for intelligence tests. *Intelligence, 15,* 79-103. (Reprinted in *Louis Guttman on theory and methodology: Selected writings,* pp. 147-171, by S. Levy, Ed., Aldershot, UK: Dartmouth)

Guttman, R., Zohar, A., Wilderman, L., & Kahnermann, I. (1988). Spouse similarities in personality traits for intra- and interethnic marriages in Israel. *Personality and Individual Differences, 9,* 763-770.

Hans, S., Bernstein, V., & Marcus, J. (1985). Some uses of the facet approach in child development. In D. Canter (Ed.), *Facet theory: Approaches to social research* (pp. 151-172). New York: Springer Verlag.

Harrelson, L. E., Jordan, J. E., & Horn, H. (1972). An application of Guttman facet theory to the study of attitudes toward the mentally retarded in Germany. *Journal of Psychology, 80,* 323-335.

Heady, B., Holmström, E., & Wearing, A. (1984). Well-being and ill-being: Different dimensions? *Social Indicators Research, 14,* 115-139.

Herzberg, F., Mausner, B., & Snyderman, B. (1958). *The motivation to work.* New York: John Wiley.

Hofstätter, P. (1966). *Einführung in die Sozialpsychologie.* [Introduction to social psychology.] Stuttgart, Germany: Kröner.

Hull, C. L. (1943). *Principles of behavior.* New York: Appleton-Century-Crofts.

Hull, C. L. (1952). *A behavior system.* New Haven, CT: Yale University Press.

Indow, T. (1974). Applications of multidimensional scaling in perception. In E. C. Carterette & M. P. Friedman (Eds.), *Handbook of perception* (Vol. 2, pp. 493-531). New York: Academic Press.

Jackson, B. B. (1983). *Multivariate data analysis.* Homewood, IL: Irwin.

James, R. C., & James, G. (1976). *Mathematics dictionary.* New York: Van Nostrand Reinhold.

Jordan, J. E. (1971). Construction of a Guttman facet designed cross-cultural attitude behavior scale toward mental retardation. *American Journal of Mental Deficiency, 76,* 201-219.

Jurgensen, C. E. (1978). Job preferences (What makes a job good or bad?). *Journal of Applied Psychology, 63,* 267-276.

Katz, D., & Kahn, R. L. (1966). *The social psychology of organizations.* New York: John Wiley.

Kernberg, O. F., Burstein, E. D., Coyne, L., Applebaum, A., Horwitz, L., & Voth, H. (1972). Psychotherapy and psychoanalysis. *Bulletin of the Menninger Clinic, 36*(No. 1/2).

Krantz, D. H., Luce, R. D., Suppes, P., & Tversky, A. (1971). *Foundations of measurement* (Vol. 1). New York: Academic Press.

Krebs, D., & Schuessler, K. (1987). *Soziale Empfindungen.* [Social life feelings.] Frankfurt, Germany: Campus.

Kruskal, J. B. (1964). Multidimensional scaling by optimizing goodness of fit to a nonmetric hypothesis. *Psychometrika, 29,* 115-129.

Levy, S. (1976). Use of the mapping sentence for coordinating theory and research: A cross-cultural example. *Quality & Quantity, 10,* 117-125.

Levy, S. (1978). Involvement as a component of attitude: Theory and political examples. In S. Shye (Ed.), *Theory construction and data analysis in the behavioral sciences* (pp. 300-324). San Francisco: Jossey Bass.

Levy, S. (1981). Lawful roles of facets in social theories. In I. Borg (Ed.), *Multidimensional data representations: When and why* (pp. 65-107). Ann Arbor, MI: Mathesis Press.

Levy, S. (1983). A cross-cultural analysis of the structure and levels of attitudes towards acts of political protest. *Social Indicators Research, 12,* 281-309.

Levy, S. (1984). Structure and dynamics of proscriptive values of Israeli high school youth. *Youth and Society, 16,* 217-235.

Levy, S. (1986). *The structure of social values.* Louis Guttman Israel Institute of Applied Social Research (Publication No. SL/917/E).

Levy, S., & Guttman, L. (1975). On the multivariate structure of wellbeing. *Social Indicators Research, 2,* 361-388.

Levy, S., & Guttman, L. (1981). Structure and level of values for rewards and allocation criteria in several life areas. In I. Borg (Ed.). *Multidimensional data representations: When and why* (pp. 153-192). Ann Arbor, MI: Mathesis Press.

Levy, S., & Guttman, L. (1985). The partial order of severity of thyroid cancer with the prognosis of survival. In J. F. Marcotorchino, J. M. Proth, & J. Jansen (Eds.), *Data analysis in real life environment: Ins and outs of solving problems* (pp. 111-119). Amsterdam: Elsevier. (Reprinted in *Louis Guttman on theory and methodology: Selected writings,* pp. 253-261, by S. Levy, Ed., Aldershot, UK: Dartmouth)

Lewin, K. (1938). *The conceptual representation and the measurement of psychological forces.* Durham, NC: Duke University Press.

Lewy, A., & Shye, S. (1978). Three main approaches to evaluating education: Analyses and comparison by facet technique. In S. Shye (Ed.), *Theory construction and data analysis in the behavioral sciences.* San Francisco: Jossey-Bass.

Lieblich, A., & Haran, S. (1969). Personal styles of reaction to the frustration of others. *Multivariate Behavioral Research, 4,* 211-222.

Lingoes, J. C. (1968). The multivariate analysis of qualitative data. *Multivariate Behavioral Research, 3,* 61-94.

Lingoes, J. C. (1973). *The Guttman-Lingoes nonmetric program series.* Ann Arbor, MI: Mathesis Press.

Lingoes, J. C. (1979). Testing regional hypotheses in multidimensional scaling. *Proceedings of the Second International Symposium on Data Analysis and Informatics.* Versailles, France: Institute de Recherche d'Informatique et d'Automatique.

Lingoes, J. C. (1981). Testing regional hypotheses in multidimensional scaling. In I. Borg (Ed.), *Multidimensional data representations: When and why* (pp. 280-310). Ann Arbor, MI: Mathesis Press.

Lingoes, J. C. (1983). Identifying regions in space for interpretation. In J. C. Lingoes (Ed.), *Geometric representations of relational data* (pp. 115-126). Ann Arbor, MI: Mathesis Press.

Lingoes, J. C., & Borg, I. (1979). Identifying spatial manifolds for interpretation. In J. C. Lingoes (Ed.), *Geometric representations of relational data* (pp. 127-148). Ann Arbor, MI: Mathesis Press.

Lingoes, J. C., & Cooper, T. (1971). PEP-I: A FORTRAN IV (G) program for Guttman-Lingoes nonmetric probability clustering. *Behavioral Science, 16,* 259-261.

Luce, R. D. (1989). R. Duncan Luce. In G. Lindzey (Ed.), *A history of psychology in autobiography* (pp. 244-289). Stanford, CA: Stanford University Press.

Luce, L. (1994). Letter in response to article by Schönemann (1994).

Marcus, J., & Hans, S. L. (1982). A methodological model to study the effects of toxins on child development. *Neurobehavioral toxicology and teratology, 4,* 483-487.

Marcus, J., Hans, S. L., Patterson, C. B., & Morris, A. J. (1983). A longitudinal study of offspring born to methadone-maintained women: I. Design, methodology and description of women's resources for functioning. In J. Marcus (Ed.), *Clinical research design and statistical analysis of individuals and subgroups* (Publication No. 1, pp. 121-153). Chicago: University of Chicago, Laboratory for Research Methodology in Child Development.

Maslow, A. H. (1954). *Motivation and personality.* New York: Harper & Row.

Meehl, P. (1978). Sir Karl, Sir Ronald, and soft psychology. *Journal of Consulting and Clinical Psychology, 46,* 806-834. (Excerpts in *On scientific thinking,* pp. 252-261, by R. D. Tweeney, M. E. Doherty, & C. R. Mynatt, Eds., 1981, New York: Columbia University Press)

Mellenbergh, G. J., Keldermann, H., Stijlen, J. G., & Zondag, E. (1979). Linear models for the analysis and construction of instruments in a facet design. *Psychological Bulletin, 86,* 766-776.

Misher, C. W., Thorne, K. S., & Wheeler, J. A. (1973). *Gravitation.* San Francisco.

Moorhead, G., & Griffin, R. W. (1989). *Organizational behavior.* Boston: Houghton Mifflin Company.

Morrison, P. (1990). The use of environmental seclusion in psychiatric settings: A multidimensional scalogram analysis. *Journal of Environmental Psychology, 10,* 353-362.

Municipality of Jerusalem & The Jerusalem Institute for Israel Studies (1992). *Statistical yearbook of Jerusalem.* Jerusalem: The Jerusalem Institute for Israel Studies.

Nelder, J. A., & Mead, R. (1965). A simplex method for function minimization. *Computer Journal, 7,* 308-313.

Nunnally, J. C. (1978). *Psychometric theory.* New York: McGraw-Hill.

Ostrom, T. M. (1969). The relationship between the affective, behavioral, and cognitive components of attitude. *Journal of Experimental and Social Psychology, 5,* 12-30.

Press, W. H., Flannery, B. P., Teukolsky, S. A., & Vetterling, W. T. (1986). *Numerical recipes.* Cambridge, UK: Cambridge University Press.

Roberts, F. S. (1979). *Measurement theory.* Reading, MA: Addison Wesley.

Rosenberg, M. J. (1957). *Occupations and values.* Glencoe, IL: Free Press.

Rossi, P. H., & Anderson, A. B. (1982). The factorial survey approach. In P. H. Rossi & S. L. Nock (Eds.), *Measuring social judgments* (pp. 14-67). Beverly Hills, CA: Sage.

Rossi, P. H., & Nock, S. L. (Eds.). (1982). *Measuring social judgments.* Beverly Hills, CA: Sage.

Rothkopf, E. Z. (1958). A measure of stimulus similarity and errors in some paired-associate learning tasks. *Journal of Experimental Psychology, 53,* 94-101.

Runkel, P. J., & MacGrath, J. E. (1968). *Research on human behavior.* New York: Holt, Rinehart & Winston.

Russett, B., & Shye, S. (1993). Aggressiveness, involvement and commitment in foreign policy attitudes. In D. Caldwell & T. J. McKeown (Eds.), *Diplomacy, force and leadership: Essays in honor of Alexander L. George* (pp. 41-60). Boulder, CO: Westview.

Schlesinger, I. M. (1978). On some properties of mapping sentences. In S. Shye (Ed.), *Theory construction and data analysis in the behavioral sciences* (pp. 181-191). San Francisco: Jossey-Bass.

Schönemann, P. H. (1981). Factorial definitions of intelligence: Dubious legacy of dogma in data analysis. In I. Borg (Ed.), *Multidimensional data representations: When and why* (pp. 325-374). Ann Arbor, MI: Mathesis Press.

Schönemann, P. H. (1994). The reasonable ineffectiveness of mathematics in the social sciences. In I. Borg & P. Ph. Mohler (Eds.), *Trends and perspectives in empirical social research* (pp. 149-160). New York: Walter DeGruyter.

Schönemann, P. H., & Borg, I. (1983). Grundlagen der metrischen mehrdimensionalen Skaliermethoden. [Foundations of metric multidimensional scaling methods.] In H. Feger & J. Bredenkamp (Eds.), *Encyclopädie der Psychologie: Messen und Testen* (pp. 257-345). Göttingen, Germany: Hogrefe.

Schuessler, K. (1982). *Measuring social life feelings.* San Francisco: Jossey-Bass.

Schwarz, S. H., & Bilsky, W. (1987). Toward a universal psychological structure of human values. *Journal of Personality and Social Psychology, 53,* 550-562.

Shalit, B. (1977). Structural ambiguity and limits to coping. *Journal of Human Stress, 3,* 32-45.

Shepard, R. N. (1981). Psychological relations and psychophysical scales: On the status of "direct" psychophysical measurements. *Journal of Mathematical Psychology, 24,* 21-57.

Sherman, C. R. (1972). Nonmetric multidimensional scaling: A Monte-Carlo study of the basic parameters. *Psychometrika, 37,* 323-355.

Shoham, S., Guttman, L., & Rahav, G. (1970). A two-dimensional space for classifying legal offenses. *Journal of Research in Crime and Delinquency, 7,* 219-243.

Shye, S. (1970). *On mapping sentences and their derivation through the use of SSA.* Jerusalem: The Israel Institute of Applied Social Research.

Shye, S. (1975). *A note on the interpretation of principal components.* Unpublished technical report. Louis Guttman Israel Institute of Applied Social Research, Jerusalem.

Shye, S. (1975). *A note on the interpretation of principal components.* Jerusalem: The Israel Institute of Applied Social Research.

Shye, S. (1978a). Achievement motive: A faceted definition and structural analysis. *Multivariate Behavioral Research, 13,* 327-346.

Shye, S. (1978b). Facet analysis and regional hypotheses. In S. Shye (Ed.), *Theory construction and data analysis in the behavioral sciences* (pp. 393-399). San Francisco: Jossey-Bass.

Shye, S. (1978c). On the search for laws in the behavioral sciences. In S. Shye (Ed.), *Theory construction and data analysis in the behavioral sciences* (pp. 2-24). San Francisco: Jossey-Bass.

Shye, S. (1978d). Partial order scalogram analysis. In S. Shye (Ed.), *Theory construction and data analysis in the behavioral sciences* (pp. 265-279). San Francisco: Jossey-Bass.

Shye, S. (Ed.). (1978e). *Theory construction and data analysis in the behavioral sciences.* San Francisco: Jossey-Bass.

Shye, S. (1982). Compiling expert opinion on the impact on environmental quality of a nuclear power plant: An application of a systemic quality of life model. *International Review of Applied Psychology, 31,* 285-302.

Shye, S. (1985a). *Multiple scaling.* Amsterdam: North-Holland.

Shye, S. (1985b). Nonmetric multivariate models for behavioral action systems. In D. Canter (Ed.), *Facet theory: Approaches to social research* (pp. 97-148). New York: Springer.

Shye, S. (1988). Inductive and deductive reasoning: A structural reanalysis of ability tests. *Journal of Applied Psychology, 73,* 308-311.

Shye, S. (1989). The systemic quality of life model: A basis for urban renewal evaluation. *Social Indicators Research, 21,* 343-378.

Shye, S. (1991a). Faceted SSA: A computer program for the PC. Jerusalem: Louis Guttman Israel Institute of Applied Social Research.

Shye, S. (1991b, June). *The integration of research content and topological space: Confirmatory SSA and LSA (new programs for the PC).* Paper presented at the Third International Facet Theory Conference, Jerusalem.

Shye, S. (1991c). What is facet theory? *Megamot, 31,* 319-330.

Shye, S. (1992). *Structural inference as a basis for assessments: Applications of the multiple scaling model to expert systems.* Jerusalem: Louis Guttman Institute of Applied Social Research.

Shye, S. (1994a). Facet theory. In T. Husen & T. N. Postlethwaite (Eds.), *International encyclopedia of education, 2nd edition* (pp. 2213-2219). Oxford: Pergamon.

Shye, S. (1994b). Partial order scalogram analysis. In T. Husen & T. N. Postlethwaite (Eds.), *International encyclopedia of education, 2nd edition* (pp. 4308-4316). Oxford: Pergamon.

Shye, S. (1994c). Smallest space analysis. In T. Husen & T. N. Postlethwaite (Eds.), *International encyclopedia of education, 2nd edition* (pp. 5497-5504). Oxford: Pergamon.

Shye S. (in press). *Decision making by expert systems: The calibration of POSAC scales.* Jerusalem: Louis Guttman Institute of Applied Social Research.

Shye, S., & Amar, R. (1985). Partial-order scalogram analysis by base coordinates and lattice mapping of the items by their scalogram roles. In D. Canter (Ed.), *Facet theory: Approaches to social research* (pp. 277-298). New York: Springer Verlag.

Shye, S., & Elizur, D. (1976). Worries about deprivation of job rewards following computerization: A partial order scalogram analysis. *Human Relations, 29,* 63-71.

Shye, S., & Elizur, D. (1988, June). *The evolution of generalized conceptual frameworks for work value structures.* Paper presented at the First International Congress on Work Values, Budapest, Hungary.

Shye, S., & Elizur, D. (with Hoffman, M.). (1994). *Introduction to facet theory.* Newbury Park, CA: Sage.

Shye, S., & Klauer, K. J. (1991). *The formalization of inductive reasoning.* Second Annual Report. Jerusalem: Louis Guttman Israel Institute of Applied Social Research.

Shye, S., & Savelzon, O. (1993, August-September). The POSAC approach to discriminant analysis for decision making and prediction. In *Proceedings of the Fourth International Facet Theory Conference, Prague,* pp. 434-442. Jerusalem, Israel: Facet Theory Association.

Snow, R. E., Kyllonen, P. C., & Marshalek, B. (1984). The topography of ability and learning correlations. In R. J. Sternberg (Ed.), *Advances in the psychology of human intelligence* (Vol. 3, pp. 47-103). Hillsdale, NJ: Lawrence Erlbaum.

Spearman, C. (1927). *The abilities of man.* New York: Macmillan. (Reprinted under same title, 1932, New York: AMS Press)

Spence, K. W. (1956). *Behavior theory and conditioning.* New Haven, CT: Yale University Press.

Suppe, F. (1973). The search for philosophic understanding of scientific theories. In F. Suppe (Ed.), *The structure of scientific theories* (pp. 1-232). Urbana, IL: University of Illinois Press.

Suppes, P., & Zinnes, J. L. (1963). Basic measurement theory. In R. D. Luce, R. R. Bush, & E. Galanter (Eds.), *Handbook of mathematical psychology* (Vol. 1, pp. 1-76). New York: John Wiley.

Takane, Y., Young, F. W., & De Leeuw, J. (1977). Nonmetric individual differences multidimensional scaling: An alternating least squares method with optimal scaling features. *Psychometrika, 42,* 7-67.

Thurstone, L. L. (1935). *The vectors of mind.* Chicago: University of Chicago Press.

Torgerson, W. S. (1958). *Theory and methods of scaling.* New York: John Wiley.

Tukey, J. W. (1987). Data analysis and behavioral sciences or learning to bear the quantitative man's burden by shunning badmandments. In L. V. Jones (Ed.), *The collected works of John W. Tukey* (Vol. 3, pp. 187-389). Monterey, CA: Wadsworth.

Tukey, J. W. (1988). *The collected works* (W. S. Cleveland, Ed.). Pacific Grove, CA: Wadsworth.

van den Wollenberg, A. L. (1978). Nonmetric representation of the radex in its factor pattern parametrization. In S. Shye (Ed.), *Theory construction and data analysis in the behavioral sciences* (pp. 326-349). San Francisco: Jossey-Bass.

Veerman, P. E. (1992). *The rights of the child and the changing image of childhood.* Dordrecht, Netherlands: Martinus Nijhoff.

Velleman, P., & Wilkinson, L. (1993). Nominal, ordinal, interval, and ratio typologies are misleading. *American Statistician, 47*(1), 65-72. (Reprinted, with some changes, in *Trends and perspectives in empirical social research,* pp. 161-177, by I. Borg & P. Ph. Mohler, Eds., 1994, New York: Walter DeGryuter)

Vroom, V. H. (1964). *Work and motivation.* New York: John Wiley.

Wagner, F., Huerkamp, M., Jockisch, H., & Graumann, C. F. (1990). *Sprachlich realisierte soziale Diskriminierungen: Empirische Überprüfungen eines Modells expliziter Diskriminierung.* [Social discrimination in language: Empirical tests of a model of explicit discrimination.] Germany, Universität Heidelberg: Arbeiten aus dem SFB 245 (Sprechen und Sprachverstehen im sozialen Kontext), Nr. 23.

Westhoff, K. (1987). The first law of concentration. *Archiv für Psychologie, 139,* 49-53.

Westhoff, K., & Kluck, M. L. (1984). Ansätze einer Theorie konzentrativer Leistungen. [Elements of a theory of concentration performance.] *Diagnostica, 30,* 167-183.

Westhoff, K., & Lemme, M. (1988). Eine erweiterte Prüfung einer Konzentrationstheorie. [An expanded study of a theory of concentration.] *Diagnostica, 3,* 244-255.

Wiggins, J. S. (1980). *Personality and prediction: Principles of personality assessment.* Reading, MA: Addison-Wesley.

Wille, R. (1982). Restructuring lattice theory: An approach based on hierarchies of concepts. In I. Rival (Ed.), *Ordered sets* (pp. 445-470). Dordrecht-Boston: Reidel.

Wish, M. (1965). A facet-theoretic approach to Morse code and related signals. Michigan Mathematical Psychology Program, MMPP 65-6.

Wolff, K. E. (1994). A first course in formal concept analysis—How to understand line diagrams. In F. Faulbaum (Ed.), *Advances in statistical software* (pp. 427-438). Stuttgart, Germany: Fischer.

Wozner, Y. (1982). Assessing the quality of international life. *Human Relations, 35,* 1059-1072.

Wozner, Y. (1991). *People care in institutions: A conceptual schema and its applications.* New York: Haworth.

Zvulun, E. (1978). Multidimensional scalogram analysis: The method and its applications. In S. Shye (Ed.). *Theory construction and data analysis in the behavioral sciences* (pp. 237-264). San Francisco: Jossey-Bass.

Index

About the Authors

Ingwer Borg is Scientific Director at ZUMA (Center for Survey Research and Methodology) and Professor of Psychology at the University of Giessen, Germany. He studied experimental psychology at Tulane (M.S.), applied psychology at Munich (Ph.D.), and mathematical psychology at Michigan (PostDoc). He was Visiting Professor at Purdue, Chicago, and Hebrew University. His research interests are mainly in psychological methodology and organizational psychology.

Samuel Shye is a Senior Research Associate at the Louis Guttman Israel Institute of Applied Social Research and Adjunct Professor at the Department of Psychology, Faculty of Social Sciences of the Hebrew University of Jerusalem, teaching facet theory and multiple scaling. He is the author of *Multiple Scaling: The Theory and Application of Partial Order Scalogram Analysis* (1985) and the editor of *Theory Construction and Data Analysis in the Behavioral Sciences* (1978). His major research interests include faceted mathematical models for behavioral systems and their application to the measurement of human quality of life, organizational quality, and other systemic concepts; the study of human inductive ability; and the modeling of heuristic expert systems. He is Secretary of the International Facet Theory Association (FTA), a member of the International Group for Chaos Studies at Ben Gurion University, and a member of the American Psychological Association.

194